CALL BACK YESTERDAYS

CALL BACK YESTERDAYS

by

Edgar Andrew Collard

LONGMANS CANADA LIMITED

Printed and bound in Canada
by McCorquodale & Blades Printers Ltd.

Acknowledgments

Many have helped me in the preparation of this book and it is a pleasure to say how grateful I am to them all.

Mr. J. Lovell Baker kindly lent me the privately printed memoirs of his grandmother, Mrs. John Lovell. I wish to thank Mr. Murray Ballantyne for lending me his transcript of the memoirs dictated by Harrison Stephens. Mr. J. Alex Edmison, Q.C., of Ottawa, has been constantly helpful in providing many old papers and other items. To Mrs. Cameron Hough I am indebted for making available to me her family scrapbook, which contained a copy of the address in 1908 of J. W. Hughes, on "How Plumbing Was Done in Montreal Fifty Years Ago". Mr. Walter Jackson provided me with the photograph of the flooded streets of Montreal. Mr. Lawrence M. Lande, apart from helping in innumerable other ways, lent me from his library of rare Canadiana his copy of *La Revue Canadienne* for 1845, and the privately printed *Recollections of Canada and the United States* by George Tuthill Borrett. Mr. W. K. Newcomb Jr. both made known to me and lent me his copy of *Harper's New Monthly Magazine* for 1889, containing C. H. Farnham's article on Montreal. To the late C. F. Notman I am grateful for lending me the memoirs of 1857 and 1858, written by his mother in 1878.

I owe much to Mrs. Florence Mary Ramsden, Mr. L. H. D. Sutherland and Mr. W. G. Radford for the manuscripts of their recollections of Victorian Montreal, all of which first appeared in my column "All Our Yesterdays" in *The Gazette*.

I acknowledge with gratitude valuable assistance from the New York Public Library, the Library of Parliament, the Toronto Public Library, the McGill University Library, the Westmount Public Library, the Fraser-Hickson Library, the Public Archives of Canada, the Archives of the Province of Quebec, the McCord Museum, and the National Gallery of Canada.

My greatest gratitude is to my wife. The sharing of interests in Canadiana has made all the work on this book a pleasure. Much that she found in her own line of research has proved of value to mine. Her discovery of Mrs. Harriet Beecher Stowe's account of her visit to Montreal in 1869 is only one example of her help, which is too full for complete enumeration or for sufficient thanks.

Contents

To Elizabeth, my wife
Quick and vivid are her ways,
Nothing dull, or blurred, or mean ...

Introduction

In this book the life of Montreal in the ninteenth century is pictured by those who lived it. The writers are of many kinds: travellers, merchants, doctors, journalists, army officers, housewives, lawyers, sportsmen, a governor-general's lady, a plumber, and a chief of police. All saw Montreal at different times, from different points of view, and wrote down their experience in different ways. The way of looking at things varies from the tourist's alert and critical observation to the old Montrealer's nostalgia for his receded youth. Some of these writers are great names in literature, as Washington Irving and Charles Dickens. Others are obscure, with no claims upon fame. Still others are even anonymous, with an identity that may never be known.

Though this is a book about Montreal, it is not only for Montrealers or for those who may once have lived in the city. It may prove of interest to all who share the growing curiosity about the manners, moods and background of the nineteenth century. For that century gave all parts of Canada much in common, and it lingers as the greatest historical presence.

Descriptions written out of experience are only one kind of historical material. Many others are needed to fill in the record; for while personal experience comes in gleams and insights, it lacks the steadier continuity and detachment that lie in the long files of official documents. But in the records of experience is a living quality to be found nowhere else. Though they may be fragmentary, they are vital.

Stephen Leacock, in his later years, used to say that

the human side of history was attracting him more and more. He found himself wondering how the past had felt for those to whom it was the present. Nor did he believe that this desire to recapture the feeling of the day-to-day life of those who once lived was without deeper meaning. "For after all," he said, "the life of an individual has in its silent passage to the end the same unfathomed meaning as the life of a nation."

Montreal of the nineteenth century was above all the city of the "two solitudes," for in that century the "two solitudes" were solidified and confirmed. French and English shared the city, but each lived largely apart. Descriptions of Montreal by most French Montrealers picture a city that might seem altogether French; those by most English Montrealers, a city altogether English. It was left to visitors to see the two cities, and to be pleased by the picturesque contrasts, or to marvel that a house so divided could still stand.

Nineteenth-century descriptions of Montreal in French are fewer than in English. The French Montrealers did not look at their city with the novelty of the many English inhabitants who had come as immigrants, saw things with fresh eyes, and made comparisons. Fewer visitors came to Montreal from France than from the British Isles or the United States. And French-Canadian writers were preoccupied with poetry, or the history of the Old Régime, or descriptions of their travels in France and Italy, or with political and religious themes. When they turned to descriptive writing, they wrote of the countryside rather than of the cities; for the life of the farm was still the ideal of French Canada, the hope of its security and survival.

Through the nineteenth century the English and the

French both asserted their presence in Montreal, but in quite different ways. The English presence was manifest in commerce and industry, in port, factory, and mansion, and (in the century's later years) in the rise of the office buildings.

The French presence was manifest in the number and awesome size of the religious buildings. Such impressive institutions as the Hôtel Dieu and the Congrégation de Notre Dame were venerable even when the century began. By the eighteen-forties the tall towers of Notre Dame Church in Place d'Armes were raised up over the whole city, in unrivalled height, and seen by travellers while yet a great way off, as their first glimpse of Montreal. And in the later years of the century, when commerce was raising pinnacles of its own, the vast St. James Cathedral at Dominion Square (first known as St. Peter's) rose up to reassert the French Catholic power.

These two assertions of presence — the commercial and the ecclesiastical — even though contrasting, were not really rivals. Each presided over its own sphere. Not even in the eighteen-sixties, when the Protestant churches clustered their spires up Beaver Hall Hill and along Dorchester Street, could the brooding ascendancy of the Roman Church be challenged. Here, again, were two solitudes, each impressive as every visitor acknowledged — separate worlds, though often near.

In compiling this book it has seemed necessary to make a distinction between descriptions of happenings and descriptions of the way of life. So many things happened in Montreal in the nineteenth century that descriptions of "events" would make a book of their own. The selections made have been confined to descriptions of how the city looked and lived. Where events have been included — as with the St. Jean Baptiste procession of 1870, or the flood of 1885, or the Winter Carnival of 1887 — this has been done because these were not unique or unusual happenings, but typical of a series and part of the Montreal scene. Nineteenth-century Montreal saw many St. Jean Baptiste processions, many floods, many Winter Carnivals.

Perhaps this collection of historical materials may prove of some value as a source-book for those interested in Montreal or the nineteenth century for other historical purposes. The selections have come from diverse sources: from travel books, newspapers, magazines, reports, books of memoirs, sporting guides, speeches, pamphlets, and manuscripts (including the manuscripts of reminiscences written for me by old Montrealers).

The sources of all selections are given fully. Each selection is presented exactly as in the original, with all the variations of spelling, the curiosities of punctuation and even the original typographical errors. The conventional "[sic]" has not been inserted after every inconsistency or mistake, as its frequency would disturb the quaintness and flavour of the original. Where an error has seemed of sufficient importance to need correction, this has been done either in the introductory passage written for the selection, or by inserting the correction within square brackets immediately after the error. Where any portion of the original text has been omitted, this has been indicated.

These contemporary descriptions often seem in surprising contrast to the appearance and the mood of Montreal today. This gives them not only greater picturesqueness but also greater relevance. For the sharp breaking away from the past — the very pace of change — may give a deeper rather than a lesser significance to a century that is both the background and the explanation of much that is happening today.

1

On the Threshold of the Century

How Montreal looked and lived as the nineteenth century was about to open was described by Isaac Weld. In July, 1796, he stayed for three weeks in lodgings in Place d'Armes. He had come as a traveller to observe and report, and everything about the quaint city interested him.

Though Montreal was set in the New World, it had much the appearance of a city of the Old World, for the impress of the French régime was still upon it. The settlers from France had built a little city in stone, and surrounded it with a fortification wall, almost as though they were reproducing the medieval narrowness of streets and their grey gloom. Though the continent spread far away, vast beyond imagination, the buildings in Montreal were huddled together, as in a town on one of the old, slow rivers of France, where land was measured minutely, and thick stone walls were raised, and all was done as though the future would never change, and everything should be made to last forever.

The old wall which defined the city from its suburbs would be roughly marked today by Fortification Lane to the north, McGill Street to the west, Berri Street to the east, and Commissioners' Street to the south. The wall had been built in the French régime by Chaussegros de Léry, the King's Engineer, and it was removed early in the nineteenth century.

The Notre Dame Church that Weld describes stood on the south side of Place d'Armes, just in front of the present church, and covering land that is now part of Notre Dame Street. It was demolished after the present church was opened for worship in 1829. The little chapel, or dead-house, where the bodies of the dead were placed before funerals, stood on land now covered by the Bank of Montreal.

Isaac Weld was one of the professional travellers — called "topographical writers" — who characterized the eighteenth and nineteenth centuries. An Irishman from Dublin, he set out in 1795 to see and describe the United States and Canada. He was well recommended and mingled in the best society; he even visited Mount Vernon and met George Washington. After his tour of the United States, he came up to Montreal by way of Lake Champlain.

The narrative of his North American travels first appeared in 1799. Few travel books of the period were more successful. It went through several English editions, as well as a French and a Dutch translation, and two German translations. In 1801 the Lord Lieutenant of Ireland asked him to prepare a pamphlet, based on his book, which would encourage emigrants to settle in Canada instead of the United States.

Weld travelled widely in later years, wrote on the topography and statistics of Ireland, and was much honoured by literary societies. He died in 1856.

His description of Montreal is taken from Chapters XXI and XXII of his *Travels through the States of North America, and the Provinces of Upper and Lower Canada, during the years 1795, 1796, and 1797* (pages 220-228 of the fourth edition, London, 1800).

Montreal is situated on an island of the same name, on the opposite side of the river St. Lawrence to that on which La Prarie stands, but somewhat lower down. The two towns are nine miles apart, and the river is about two miles and a quarter wide. The current here is prodigiously strong, and in particular places as you cross, the boats are hurried down the stream, in the midst of large rocks, with such impetuosity, that it seems as if nothing could save them from being dashed to pieces; indeed this would certainly be the case if the men were not uncommonly expert; but the Canadians are the most dexterous people perhaps in the world at the management of bateaux in rapid rivers. After such a prospect of the River St. Lawrence, it was not without astonishment that, on approaching the town of Montreal, we beheld ships of upwards of four hundred tons burthen lying close to the shore. The difficulties which vessels have to encounter in getting into Montreal are immense; I have myself seen them with all their sails set, and with a smart and favourable breeze, stationary for an hour together in the stream, unable to stem it, between the island of St. Helene and the main land, just below the town: to stem the current at this place it is almost necessary that the vessel should be aided by a storm. The ascent is equally difficult in several other parts of the river. Owing to this it is, that the passage from Quebec to Montreal is generally more tedious than that across the Atlantic; those ships, therefore, which trade between Europe and Montreal, never attempt to make more than one voyage during the year. Notwithstanding the rapidity of the stream, the channel of the river is very deep, and in particular just opposite to the town. The largest merchant vessels can there lie so close to the banks, which are in their natural state, that you may nearly touch them with your hand as you stand on the shore. . . .

The town at present contains about twelve hundred houses, whereof five hundred only are within the walls; the rest are in the suburbs, which commence from the north, east, and west gates. The houses in the suburbs are mostly built of wood, but the others are all of stone; none of them are elegant, but there are many very comfortable habitations. In the lower part of the town, towards the river, where most of the shops stand, they have a very gloomy appearance, and look like so many prisons, being all furnished at the outside with sheet iron shutters to the doors and windows, which are regularly closed towards evening, in order to guard against fire. The town has suffered by fire very materially at different times, and the inhabitants have such a dread of it, that all who can afford it cover the roofs of their houses with tin-plates instead of shingles. By law they are obliged to have one or more ladders, in proportion to the size of the house, always ready on the roofs.

The streets are all very narrow; three of them run parallel to the river, and these are intersected by others at right angles, but not at regular distances. On the side of the town farthest from the river, and nearly between the northern and southern extremities, there is a small square, called La Place d'Armes, which seems originally to have been left open to the walls on one side, and to have been intended for the military to exercise in; the troops, however, never make use of it now, but parade on a long walk, behind the walls, nearer to the barracks. On the opposite side of the town, towards the water, is another small square, where the market is held.

There are six churches in Montreal; one for English Episcopalians, one for Presbyterians, and four for Roman Catholics. The cathedral church belonging to the latter, which occupies one side of La Place d'Armes, is a very spacious building, and contains five altars, all very richly decorated. The doors of this cathedral are left open the greater part of the day, and there are, generally, numbers of old people in it at their prayers, even when no regular service is going on. On a fine Sunday in the summer season such multitudes flock to it, that even the steps at the outside are covered with people, who, unable to get in, remain there kneeling, with their hats off, during the whole time of divine service. Nearly all the christenings, marriages, and burials of the Roman Catholic inhabitants of Montreal, are performed in this church, on which occasions, as well as before and during the masses, they always ring the bells, to the great annoyance of every person that is not a lover of discords; for instead of pulling the bells, which are five in number, and really well toned, with regularity, they jingle them all at once, without any sort of cadence whatever. Our lodgings happened to be in La Place d'Armes; and during three weeks that we remained there, I verily believe the bells were never suffered to remain still for two hours together, at any one time, except in the night.

The funerals, as in other Roman Catholic countries, are conducted with great ceremony; the corpse is always attended to the church by a number of priests chanting prayers, and by little boys in white robes and black caps carrying wax lights. A morning scarcely ever passed over that one or more of these processions did not pass under our windows whilst we were at breakfast; for on the opposite side of the square to that on which the cathedral stood, was a sort of chapel, to which the bodies of all those persons, whose friends could not afford to pay for an expensive funeral, were brought, I suppose, in the night, for we could never see any carried in there, and from thence conveyed in the morning to the cathedral. . . .

The walls round the city are mouldering away very fast, and in some places are totally in ruins; the gates, however, remain quite perfect. The walls were built principally as a defence against the Indians, by whom the country was thickly inhabited when Montreal was founded ... When the large fairs used to be held in Montreal, to which the Indians from all parts resorted with their furs, they were also found extremely useful, as the inhabitants were thereby enabled to shut out the Indians at night, who, had they been suffered to remain in the town, addicted as they are to drinking, might have been tempted to commit great outrages, and would have kept the inhabitants in a continual state of alarm. In their best state the walls could not have protected the town against cannon, not even against a six pounder. ...

By far the greater number of the inhabitants of Montreal are of French extraction; all the eminent merchants, however, and principal people in the town, are either English, Scotch, Irish, or their descendants, all of whom pass for English with the French inhabitants. The French retain, in a great measure, the manners and customs of their ancestors, as well as the language; they have an unconquerable aversion to learn English, and it is very rare to meet with any person amongst them that can speak it in any tolerable manner; but the English inhabitants are, for the most part, well acquainted with the French language.

The people of Montreal, in general, are remarkably hospitable and attentive to strangers; they are sociable also amongst themselves, and fond in the extreme of convivial amusements. In winter, they keep up such a constant and friendly intercourse with each other, that it seems then as if the town were inhabited but by one large family. During summer they live somewhat more retired; but throughout that season a club, formed of all the principal inhabitants, both male and female, meet every week or fortnight, for the purpose of dining at some agreeable spot in the neighbourhood of the town. . . .

Two stewards are appointed for the day, who always chuse some new spot where there is a spring or rill of water, and an agreeable shade; each family brings cold provisions, wine, &c.; the whole is put together, and the company, often amounting to one hundred persons, sits down to dinner.

The fur trade is what is chiefly carried on at Montreal . . . This very lucrative trade is carried on, partly by what is called the North-west Company, and partly by private individuals on their own account. The company does not possess any particular privileges by law, but from its great capital merely it is enabled to trade to certain remote parts of the continent, to the exclusion of those who do not hold any shares in it. . . .

The canoes are navigated by the French Canadians, who are particularly fond of the employment, preferring it in general to that of cultivating the ground. A fleet of them sets off from Montreal about the month of May, laden with provisions, consisting chiefly of biscuit and salt pork, sufficient to last the crews till their return, and also with the articles given in barter to the Indians.

2

"Lords of the Ascendant"

The nearness and reality of the wilderness in the life of
Montreal appear vividly in the description of the city in
1817 by the English traveller, John Palmer. Not far from
Montreal, to the north-west, the wilderness began; and
constant reminders of what it meant to the city were given
by the manners, customs and riches of the fur trade, and the
sight of the Indians in the streets and along the shore nearby.
The Indians were to be long a feature of Montreal, but they
lost their forest wildness as the century moved on, and grew
fewer as the streets grew busier. In John Palmer's time they
still showed how close to the wilderness the city lay, for they
had their faces painted, and wore feathers and "pendulous
ear-rings."

The coming variety of commerce and the brisk industrialism
had not yet transformed Montreal. The city remained small
and curious, still much as Isaac Weld had pictured it. Boatmen sang on the river, canoes arrived at the waterfront, ships
loaded skins and furs, windmills turned their sails in the
breeze, dogs drew carts, and women washed their clothes by
the river, beating them on the rocks.

Little is known about John Palmer, but when his travel
book appeared it was praised for its observant common sense.
He seems to have been a native of Lynn in Norfolk, and when

he sailed for the United States and Canada he had as companions the English writer and political radical, William Cobbett, and Cobbett's two sons. Palmer's book was described by *The Edinburgh Review* (in an article by Rev. Sydney Smith) as having been written by a "plain man, of good sense and slow judgment," and *The British Review* described Palmer as "a sensible and observant traveller."

Palmer's description has a sharp focus, explained, perhaps, by the fact that he was not writing from memory, but was, as he says, copying "almost *verbatim*" from his notebook. The era when Montreal was dominated by the North West Company and the fur trade was soon to end; Palmer caught his impressions before its downfall.

This selection is from pages 210-13, 216-18 of his book *Journal of Travels in the United States of North America and in Lower Canada, performed in the Year 1817 ...* (London, 1818).

We arrived at Laprairie, which is a considerable place, about dusk, and there being fifty or sixty travellers, who wished to proceed immediately to Montreal, distant but nine miles across the St. Lawrence, we hired two batteaux, for twenty-five cents each person, and forthwith embarked on the bosom of that noble river. The evening was fine, and a full moon shone upon the most picturesque night scenery I had ever beheld. The rowers sung in chorus a French song, at the end of each stanza pausing, whilst the steersman took it up; they kept exact time with their oars, as did the steersman with his paddle; these boats are always steered with a paddle, in the Indian manner. After an hour and a half's rowing we arrived at Montreal, whose shining metal roofs had long presented themselves to our eyes, in company with several Americans I put up at Pomeroy's Montreal Hotel, near the principal landing; board one dollar and a quarter per day. Here a dollar passes for five, and an eagle for fifty shillings sterling. . . .

The number of inhabitants I should estimate at 15,000; they are increasing daily, if we may judge from the quantity of houses building in different streets. The people are a mixture of Canadians, British, and Americans. There are several good taverns, and the stores are full of European and India goods: they contain also a variety of articles for the trade with the Indians. Auctions of cargoes are frequent as in the States. Some few manufactures are established; amongst others, a windmill, with horizontal sails, for grinding colours or oil, and several breweries: two or three windmills for flour are in the suburbs; I saw none in the States.

Montreal is the emporium of the North West Company, the most extensive fur company in America; their forts, or trading establishments, extend some thousands of miles west to the Pacific Ocean. I was informed by one of the company, Mr. Vandersluys, that fifteen hundred people are employed by them at these establishments. The Ewereta, a large ship for London, was at Market Wharf, loading entirely with skins and furs, which are brought down the interior rivers by Indians and whites, in the service of the Company. The morning after I came here, six or eight large canoes, manned by at least eight Indians each, and loaded with peltry, arrived. The Indians were dressed in all their finery: blue leggings, trimmed with scarlet list, a gay printed shirt, or black or common blanket thrown over their shoulders, and a gaudy yarn sash round their waists; some had their faces painted red and black, &c.; some had plates of silver on, or feathers, and different animals' tails stuck in their hats, and almost all had pendulous ear-rings. The women were dressed nearly the same, excepting some of the ornaments in the hat, and I observed almost all wore a black blanket and crucifix. . . .

The country people and common people are a curious looking set of men, they are short in stature; their dress is trowsers, and mocasins, or large boots of undressed leather, a frock coat or jacket, and greasy red cap; a short pipe is always an accompaniment, whether attending the market, driving a cart, or pursuing any other avocation; many of them wear comfortables, or yarn sashes round their waists, in the manner of the Indians. In their dress the better sort of inhabitants are genteel, and they live expensively. They have few amusements, except in the winter, when all trade, or thought of it, is laid aside, and a round of pleasure ensues: visiting, tea and dinner parties, sleighing, (the sleigh is called a cariole) dances; and sometimes a concert, or scenic representation, present their irresistible attractions. Curling matches are sometimes made. There is good duck and snipe shooting in the vicinity of Montreal, and plenty of deer some way in the country. Some of the members of the North West Company have established a convivial society, called the Beaver Club, in which the calamut, or pipe of peace, is handed round, and the Indian manners, customs, and language, closely imitated. The members generally stand, but visitors have the privilege of sitting.

I saw several French-Canadian Marriages, which, I believe, from some superstition, are always on Monday: they have a train of cabriolets, a clumsy sort of gig, according to the respectability or wealth of the happy pair; on returning the bride rides first, and far from appearing reserved on the occasion, she calls out to her acquaintance in the street, or waves her handkerchief in passing them;

the market people, whom they take care to pass, greet them with shouts, which the party seem to court and enjoy.

The carts used here are light, and the body of the drays have a fall from the shafts, in the manner of our tumbrels. The horses are small; bells are fixed to their harness. Carts drawn by dogs are common; I have seen a tandem dog cart, the dogs harnessed and belled the same as horses.

The inhabitants have several proposed plans for beautifying the city, some of which will no doubt be adopted, as there is considerable riches and public spirit in the inhabitants. The old walls built round the city in the early part of its growth, to protect it from the Indians, are removed; other improvements are making, and a new street and market at the west end of St. Paul's Street is building.

The manner of washing pursued by many of the women is similar to that pursued in the West Indies. I every day saw thirty or forty soldiers' wives, and other women, standing up to their knees in water in different parts of the river, washing and beating the clothes on large stones, that lay conveniently for that purpose on the margin.

I several times walked to a small encampment of miserable Indians, who had erected temporary *wigwams*, about half a mile west of Montreal; they were about the size of a pig stye, a man could not stand upright in them; their fire for cooking was made outside the huts. I observed their victuals were the offal of the market. In trying to converse with them I was always answered "Je ne parlez Angloise." I cannot converse in French, and consequently was foiled in my attempts; this occurred to me several times in asking questions of the Canadians, when the same kind of answer was given. I am told these Indians seldom will converse with one unknown to them, who speaks English, even if they understand the language, whereas one who speaks French, to whom they are most partial, is sure to be answered with the utmost civility.

At the opening of the nineteenth century the Nor'Westers were the "lords of the ascendant" in the life of Montreal. The city had long traditions and skills in the fur trade, going back far into the French régime. All these were now gathered up by the Nor'Westers, and given vaster scope and more furious energy.

The Nor'Westers were Scots for the most part, with pride of wealth and power. At first they had carried on the trade in competition with one another. But competition proved not only wasteful, but too fragmented for the sort of continental enterprise that the fur trade had become, especially as the traders in Montreal faced the rivalry of the Hudson's Bay Company.

As early as 1779 the Nor'Westers had formed a sort of partnership, and in 1784 the North West Company came into real existence. Consolidated by several subsequent agreements, it carried out the fur trade from Lake Superior to the Pacific, and from the sources of the Mississippi to the Arctic Ocean.

Unlike the Hudson's Bay Company, the North West Company did not operate under a charter. It was a syndicate, or pool, of fur-trading firms and individuals. Being a partnership, the members lost none of their keen self-interest, and all made the most of their initiative to promote its success. They also retained a sense of personal achievement. In Montreal they lived lavishly, making winter a round of dinners and costly displays. Every year a few of the leading partners made a canoe journey into the wilderness to the company's headquarters at Fort William. They travelled in regal dignity and varied their serious councils with "huge feasts and revels."

The Nor'Westers in the days of their splendour were pictured by one of the greatest descriptive writers of the century — Washington Irving, the author of *The Sketch Book.* He was writing of what he knew, for in the early years of the century, when a young man, he had been several times in Montreal on business, and had "sat at the hospitable boards of the mighty Northwesters."

Washington Irving wrote of the Nor'Westers in Montreal in his book on John Jacob Astor and the fur trade, *Astoria, or Anecdotes of an Enterprise Beyond the Rocky Mountains,* first published in 1836. This selection appears in Chapter I (on pages 14-19 in Volume I of G. P. Putnam's edition, New York and London, 1897).

As to the principal partners, or agents, who resided in Montreal and Quebec, they formed a kind of commercial aristocracy, living in lordly and hospitable style. Their early associations when clerks at the remote trading posts, and the pleasures, dangers, adventures, and mishaps which they had shared together in their wild wood life, had linked them heartily to each other, so that they formed a convivial fraternity. Few travellers that have visited Canada some thirty years since, in the days of the M'Tavishes, the M'Gillivrays, the M'Kenzies, the Frobishers, and the other magnates of the Northwest, when the company was in all its glory, but must remember the round of feasting and revelry kept up among these hyperborean nabobs.

Sometimes one or two partners, recently from the interior posts, would make their appearance in New York, in the course of a tour of pleasure and curiosity. On these occasions there was always a degree of magnificence of the purse about them, and a peculiar propensity to expenditure at the goldsmith's and jeweller's for rings, chains, brooches, necklaces, jewelled watches, and other rich trinkets, partly for their own wear, partly for presents to their female acquaintances; a gorgeous prodigality, such as was often to be noticed in former times in Southern planters and West India creoles, when flush with the profits of their plantations.

To behold the Northwest Company in all its state and grandeur, however, it was necessary to witness an annual gathering at the great interior place of conference established at Fort William, near what is called the Grand Portage, on Lake Superior. Here two or three of the leading partners from Montreal proceeded once a year to meet the partners from the various trading posts of the wilderness, to discuss the affairs of the company during the preceding year, and to arrange plans for the future.

On these occasions might be seen the change since the unceremonious times of the old French traders; now the aristocratical character of the Briton shone forth magnificently, or rather the feudal spirit of the Highlander. Every partner who had charge of an interior post, and a score of retainers at his command, felt like the chieftain of a Highland clan, and was almost as important in the eyes of his dependants as of himself. To him a visit to the grand conference at Fort William was a most important event, and he repaired there as to a meeting of parliament.

The partners from Montreal, however, were the lords of the ascendant; coming from the midst of luxuries and ostentatious life, they quite eclipsed their compeers from the woods, whose forms and faces had been battered and hardened by hard living and hard service, and whose garments and equipments were all the worse for wear. Indeed, the partners from below considered the whole dignity of the company as represented in their persons, and conducted themselves in suitable style. They ascended the rivers in great state, like sovereigns making a progress; or rather like Highland chieftains navigating their subject lakes. They were wrapped in rich furs, their huge canoes freighted with every convenience and luxury, and manned by Canadian *voyageurs*, as obedient as Highland clansmen. They carried up with them cooks and bakers, together with delicacies of every kind, and abundance of choice wines for the banquets which attended this great convocation. Happy were they, too, if they could meet with some distinguished stranger; above all, some titled member of the British nobility, to accompany them on this stately occasion, and grace their high solemnities.

Fort William, the scene of this important annual meeting, was a considerable village on the banks of Lake Superior. Here, in an immense wooden building, was the great council hall, as also the banqueting chamber, decorated with Indian arms and accoutrements, and the trophies of the fur trade. The house swarmed at this time with traders and *voyageurs*, some from Montreal, bound to the interior posts; some from the interior posts, bound to Montreal. The councils were held in great state, for every member felt as if sitting in parliament, and every retainer and dependant looked up to the assemblage with awe, as to the House of Lords. There was a vast deal of solemn deliberation, and hard Scottish reasoning, with an occasional swell of pompous declamation.

These grave and weighty councils were alternated by huge feasts and revels, like some of the old feasts described in Highland castles. The tables in the great banqueting room groaned under the weight of game of all kinds; of venison from the woods, and fish from the lakes, with hunters' delicacies, such as buffaloes' tongues and beavers' tails, and luxuries from Montreal, all served up by experienced cooks brought for the purpose. There was no stint of generous wine, for it was hard-drinking period, a time of loyal toasts, and bacchanalian songs, and brimming bumpers.

While the chiefs thus revelled in hall, and made the rafters resound with bursts of loyalty and old Scottish songs, chanted in voices cracked and sharpened by the northern blast, their merriment was echoed and prolonged by a mongrel legion of retainers, Canadian *voyageurs,* half-breeds, Indian hunters, and vagabond hangers-on who feasted sumptuously without on the crumbs that fell from their table, and made the welkin ring with old French ditties, mingled with Indian yelps and yellings.

Such was the Northwest Company in its powerful and prosperous days, when it held a kind of feudal sway over a vast domain of lake and forest. We are dwelling too long, perhaps, upon these individual pictures, endeared to us by the associations of early life, when as yet a stripling youth, we have sat at the hospitable boards of the "mighty North-westers," the lords of the ascendant at Montreal, and gazed with wondering and inexperienced eye at the baronial wassailing, and listened with astonished ear to their tales of hardships and adventures. It is one object of our task, however, to present scenes of the rough life of the wilderness, and we are tempted to fix these few memorials of a transient state of things fast passing into oblivion; — for the feudal state of Fort William is at an end; its council chamber is silent and deserted; its banquet hall no longer echoes to the burst of loyalty, or the "auld world" ditty; the lords of the lakes and forests have passed away; and the hospitable magnates of Montreal — where are they?

Much of "village primitiveness" still lingered about Montreal when Thomas Storrow Brown arrived in 1818, a boy of fifteen, from New Brunswick. Families would sit out on their doorsteps of an evening, and at a family dance a respectable passer-by might be asked to come in. Trade was brisk in the shipping season, but froze with Montreal's wintry isolation, when clerks could devote themselves to "frolic and jollity." This sense of a primitively organized society is seen in Brown's picture of old night watchmen crying out the hours on the street corners and fires being fought with a line of leather buckets passed from hand to hand from the river.

Brown's account is also of interest as he deals with the relations of French and English in Montreal in that early period. He had supported the French-Canadian claims in the paper, the *Vindicator*, which he had helped to found in 1832, and he was one of the very few English-speaking citizens who threw in their lot with the *Patriotes* in the Rebellion of 1837. He was the "general" of the *Patriote* army when it fought the British troops under Colonel Wetherall at St. Charles on the Richelieu. After the battle, he fled to the United States and did not return to Montreal till 1844. His considerable business interests had been ruined by his political involvement, but he re-established himself in the hardware trade. He died in Montreal in 1888.

His picture of Montreal reveals a mind active and perceptive, with unusual descriptive powers. It appeared under the title "Montreal in 1818," in *The New Dominion Monthly*, Montreal, March, 1870.

I came into the city through a narrow passage leading to the Custom House Square, then the "Old Market," a low wooden shed-like building; and along the south side of the square was a row of old women seated at tables with eatables for sale. Capital street was a succession of drinking-houses, carrying on an active business from morning till night; for in those ante-temperance days drinking appeared one great object of life and daily occupation. The largest was that of *Thomas l'Italien* (Thomas Delvecchio), facing the market, with a clock on which small figures came out to strike the hours, to the continued wonderment of all; and next came *Les trois Rois*, of Joseph Donegani, the sign bearing a painting of three uncouth figures to represent the "three kings," or, as we call them, "wise men of the East." This was the centre of trade. . . .

Workmen were trenching the streets to remove logs, that had conducted water from the Mountain, to replace them with iron pipes that were to distribute water from a reservoir on the Citadel, pumped there by an engine below the Bonsecours Church, where we had all the advantages of the city sewage. What with digging for water-pipes and gas-pipes these poor streets have had little rest from that day. On removal of the Citadel the reservoir was two tanks, each about thirty feet square, occupying the third story of two dwelling-houses, still standing opposite the Donegani Hotel. While this was going on, and in all times previously, each household had a puncheon which was filled daily with water brought in carts from the river. Such for many years was our water supply. Every house was supplied with leather buckets, and, when fires occurred, they were handed out, the citizens formed in two lines to the river, one to send empty buckets down and the other to return full buckets, and thus the engines were supplied. There were some wells in town with water unfit for any use; but good water was obtained from a pump in the centre of the Place d'Armes, and another on Notre Dame street, at the west end of the Court House, opposite the house of one of our most respected and wealthiest citizens, Mr. David David, who was known to the Canadians as *le gros Juif contre le pompe* (the great Jew near the pump.) . . .

All the houses in Notre Dame street were dwellings —

in its whole length there were but two shops, and three auction rooms. The cross streets' buildings were nearly all dwellings and Commercial business was almost confined to St. Paul street. Wholesale stores, except the establishment of Gillespie, Moffat & Co., were small indeed compared to the growth of after years; and judging now from the few places where fine goods were retailed, and their smallness, the "girls of the period" must have been content with adornments that would only satisfy a somewhat indigent class of the present day. But there were numerous shops for country trade, all doors and no windows, always open Winter and Summer, with a goodly portion of the stock displayed outside, where, till within about twenty-five years, salesmen without number were stationed to accost and bring in customers, who were often dragged forcibly. The excitment on market days between these vociferous sellers, and wary buyers, pulled into one shop after another, made St. Paul street lively....

Our garrison was one regiment of infantry, then the 37th, Col. Buren, and a company of foot artillery, with a small engineer commissariat and storekeeping staff, military and naval. We had no police; but at nights old men placed at street corners as watchmen, with long blue constables' batons in their hands, shouted "all's well" at the end of every hour. The pay of officials being proportionally larger in comparison with the cost of living and ordinary incomes, made them of more consequence than in later years, and they gave themselves more airs of superiority. There were horses and carriages to be had at livery stables, but no public vehicles on the streets, except carts and trucks. Canadians used the old clumsy *caleche*, with big wings, sticking out over the wheels, and four-wheeled carriages were about being introduced. A few years earlier there was but one in the city — that of Mrs. Gregory who lived in the large stone house near our water-works. I have before named the small space in which our citizens resided. New Years' calls were soon made as they were from house to house, and no sleigh was required. . . .

We had no Corporation or city government, but magistrates and certain public functionaries ruled our city affairs with little restraint upon the citizens. When a widow or widower got married, a *charivari* was got up. Night after night a procession of masqueraders in every grotesque attire was formed, carrying torches and trans-parencies, horns, and every vile instrument of noise, to serenade the newly married, and crowds were out to see the fun. On one occasion a *charivari* lasted nightly for a month. Many of the masqueraders were mounted, and richly caparisoned; and, defying authority, assembled be-fore dark.

The first ships from sea arrived at Quebec about the same date as now, and the strong east winds frequently brought traders early to Montreal. I have often seen them discharging on the ice. One I remember arrived under sail on the fourth of May.

Spring trade commenced about the first of June, and Fall trade about the first of October, to end early in Nov-ember; after which we had a six months' holiday in trade. Though there was a few days' work in sending off *traineau* (Canadian sleigh) loads as far as Brockville or Perth, or up the Ottawa, there were no railroads or telegraphs to keep merchants and their clerks under whip and spur all the time. Mechanics waited for Spring to work. On the other hand, there being no care and little occupation during winter, all would devote themselves to frolic and jollity, in which merchants' clerks indulged so freely that I at this moment remember less than six of all the young men and lads I then knew, who have survived the consequences. Their's was a short and merry life, ending too often before the age of thirty. . . .

Village primitiveness had not disappeared in Montreal fifty years ago. Old men sat out on the door steps to gossip with passing friends, and often the family would be found there of an evening. In the suburbs, neighbors would collect for a dance in the largest house, and any respectable passer-by was welcomed if he chose to step in. In the afternoon le Sieur Berichon might be seen seated on his doorstep in St. Francois Xavier street, a representative of the *bourgeoisie* in the neatest of black coats, breeches, and cotton stockings, while as representative of the *gentilhomme* le Docteur Bender was promenading in front of his one story house in Notre Dame street, opposite the Recollet Church, glorious in powdered hair, snuff-colored coat, ruffles, silk stockings, and gold-headed cane. . . .

Business relations were more intimate between French and English fifty years ago than now, and I think there was more kindly feeling. There were then comparatively few Irish or other European mechanics or laborers in the city, and no Canadians (French) in the importing or wholesale trade (the late Mr. Masson was partner in a Scotch house); but social relations were much as they now are, the races keeping separate in their charities, their amusements, and their gatherings. The English were more predominant — they were more generally the employers — the French the employed. In public offices throughout the Province a great majority of the places were filled by English names, and the salaries of the few held by the French were, generally speaking, comparatively trifling. In 1820 there were 135 persons in the Province of Lower Canada with English names, having salaries amounting to 25,374 pounds sterling and 82 with French names, drawing salaries of only 9,961 pounds sterling, while the population of the Province was more than three-fourths French. The rise of this French element in wealth, business importance and influence in trade in the city, since the establishment of the Banque du Peuple in 1834, and the change produced by the events in 1837, are wonderful to those who can remember their depression up to that time. But the races amalgamate or intermarry as little as ever; and after a century of British rule, and a large infusion of the British races into Lower Canada — now the Province of Quebec — they exist, though intermixed, as separate people, and French nationality was never since the conquest so defined or positive as now, nor had the Roman Catholic Church ever a greater hold upon the people.

William McGillivray was the supreme host of the North West Company. He had become the company's head on the death of his uncle, Simon McTavish, in 1804, and in his mansion, St. Antoine House, he gave his dinners to visitors. He presided at his table (a huge mahogany table that could seat a score of guests without difficulty) as "a large, handsome man, with the pleasant, successful look of the men of his habits and mode of life."

His estate of some two hundred acres sloped toward the river, near what is now Guy Street. St. Antoine House, a Georgian mansion, was set on a high terrace, looking southwards, with the land round about it laid out "in pleasure-grounds in the English style."

A description of one of William McGillivray's dinners was given by Dr. John Jeremiah Bigsby, about the year 1819. Dr. Bigsby was born in Nottingham, graduated in medicine

from Edinburgh University, and joined the Army as a
medical officer. After service at the Cape, he was sent to
Canada in 1818. He took a keen interest in geology, and in
1819 was commissioned to report on the geology of Upper
Canada. In 1822 he was appointed British Secretary and
medical officer of the commission that was to determine the
boundary between Canada and the United States under the
terms of the Treaty of Ghent (the treaty that ended the War
of 1812). Five years later Dr. Bigsby returned to England,
where he practised medicine in Nottinghamshire and in
London. He died in London in 1881.

Dr. Bigsby said of St. Antoine House that it was "extremely
fine, too rich and fair, I foolishly thought, to be out of my
native England." William McGillivray had been a widower
since 1811 and he was living in the house with his two
daughters. At the table Dr. Bigsby sat beside a plain man,
plainly dressed — David Thompson, the first white man to
descend the Columbia River from its source to its mouth and
the greatest map-maker of the North-west. The conversation
at the table was about the lore of the North-west, and in the
drawing-room after dinner one of the guests sang a wild
voyageur song.

This opulent ease was near its end. The North West
Company was disintegrating, and in 1821 it was to surrender
to the Hudson's Bay Company in what was called a merger.
"I was the first English Clerk engaged in the Service of the
N.W. Co. on its first Establishment in 1784," McGillivray
wrote in a farewell letter to the Reverend John Strachan,
"and I have put my Hand and Seal to the Instrument which
closes its *career* and *name* in 1821 — "

Dr. Bigsby had seen the splendour just before it faded.
His account of that dinner is in his book *The Shoe and Canoe*
... (London, 1850), Volume I, pages 112-15, 119-22. (Foot-
notes on pages 120-22 have been omitted.)

Mr. M'Gillvray was accustomed to entertain the succes-
sive governors in their progresses, and was well entitled to
such honour, not only from his princely fortune, but from
his popularity, honesty of purpose, and intimate acquaintance with the true interests of the colony.

I hope to betray no family secrets in the following little sketch of the doings at the dinner-party.

My host was then a widower, with two agreeable and well-educated daughters. The company was various, and consisted of a judge or two, some members of the legislative council, and three or four retired partners of the North-west Company of Fur-traders. Our dinner and wines were perfect. The conversation was fluent and sensible, far above my sphere at first, about large estates, twenty to thirty miles long, and how to improve them by draining, damming, road-making, and so forth — operations only in the power of great capitalists who can wait for returns.

For myself, a young man, I listened meekly as *"de profundis;"* but at length the talk turned to a subject more attractive — the Indian fur countries, on whose frontiers I was about to wander.

I was well placed at table, between one of the Miss M——'s and a singular-looking person of about fifty. He was plainly dressed, quiet, and observant. His figure was short and compact, and his black hair was worn long all round, and cut square, as if by one stroke of the shears, just above the eyebrows. His complexion was of the gardener's ruddy brown, while the expression of his deeply-furrowed features was friendly and intelligent, but his cut-short nose gave him an odd look. His speech betrayed the Welshman, although he left his native hills when very young.

I might have been spared this description of Mr. David Thompson by saying he greatly resembled Curran the Irish orator.

He was astronomer, first, to the Hudson's Bay Company, and then to the Boundary Commission. I afterwards travelled much with him, and have now only to speak of him with great respect, or, I ought to say, with admiration.

No living person possesses a tithe of his information respecting the Hudson's Bay countries, which from 1793 to 1820 he was constantly traversing. Never mind his Bunyan-like face and cropped hair; he has a very powerful mind, and a singular faculty of picture-making. He can create a wilderness and people it with warring savages, or climb the Rocky Mountains with you in a snow-storm, so clearly and palpably, that only shut your eyes and you hear the crack of the rifle, or feel the snow-flakes melt on your cheeks as he talks.

The two other north-westers were elderly, business-like Scotchmen, strong-featured and resolute. . . . The rest of the evening was passed, to my great content, in listening to the tales . . . by one or other of the company. . . .

The guests at the wine table now joined the ladies for coffee, when one of the Miss M'Gillvray called to Mr. M———, and insisted upon his singing a wild *voyageur* song, "Le premier jour de Mai," playing the spirited tune on the piano at the same time with one hand.

Thus commanded, Mr. M——— sang it as only the true *voyageur* can do, imitating the action of the paddle, and in their high, resounding, and yet musical tones. His practised voice enabled him to give us the various swells and falls of sounds upon the waters, driven about by the winds, dispersed and softened in the wide expanses, or brought close again to the ear by neighbouring rocks. He finished, as is usual, with the piercing Indian shriek.

When this was over, and the lady had obeyed a call to the piano frankly and well, a gentleman asked Mr. M'Gill-vray what truth there was in the accounts of the dancing pheasants in the north-west, adding, that although he was at first incredulous, he could scarcely remain so after Mr. Gould's statements respecting the pastimes of the bower-bird of Australia.

Here our friend Mr. Thompson said he had repeatedly stumbled upon what might be called a "pheasants' ball," among the glades on the eastern flanks of the Rocky Mountains. In those grassy countries the almost noiseless tread of the horses' feet (unshod) sometimes is not noticed by the busy birds; but the intruder must not be seen.

"The pheasants choose a beech," said Mr. T. "for the dance, a tree with boughs, several on the same level, and only full leafed at their ends. The feathered spectators group around. Six or seven pheasants step on the trembling stage, and begin to stamp, and prance, and twinkle their little feet like so many Bayadères, skipping with *balancez et chassez* from bough to bough; or they sit with curtsey and flutter, arching their glowing necks, and opening and closing their wings in concert; but, in truth, the dance is indescribable, most singular, and laughable. When it has lasted ten minutes, a new set of performers step forward, and the exhibition may last a couple of hours."

I confess to have been at the time greatly staggered by this story; but we see it has been verified, as well as another as incredible, from the same gentleman. He told us that in the far north-west, near the Arctic circle, the ice forms over a river, and the water sometimes deserts its bed. There is a dry channel, with a high arch of rough ice overhead, tinted white, green, and earth-coloured, if the banks are lofty. He said he had travelled for the best part of a mile in such a tunnel, simply because it was the best road.

It is hardly necessary to say that I passed a very agreeable evening. Our host was a large, handsome man, with the pleasant, successful look of the men of his habits and mode of life. I hope that what entertained me will entertain others.

It is perhaps a little strange that one of the most poetical descriptions of Montreal should have been written by a scientist. But Benjamin Silliman, the Professor of Chemistry at Yale and a pioneer in scientific education in North America, had a mind quite as ready to receive poetical impressions as to seek definable facts. He travelled widely, and always in a receptive spirit, observing and enjoying rather than criticizing and rejecting.

In 1805, he began a tour of fourteen months in England and on the European continent, and his record of his experiences was well received on both side of the Atlantic. His narrative of a second tour, made in 1851, was so popular that it reached six editions.

Prof. Silliman came to Montreal in the autumn of 1819 and, after a rough passage across the St. Lawrence when the canoe was pulled about in St. Mary's Current between St. Helen's Island and Montreal, he put up at the Mansion House. This hotel on St. Paul Street (occupying what is now the east end of the Bonsecours Market) provided him with rooms whose windows and terrace looked out over the waterfront.

This waterfront view fascinated him. Turning away from the cruder side of the Montreal scene, which other travellers had depicted, Prof. Silliman simply enjoyed the night and day tableaux framed for him by the Mansion House windows.

This passage is from pages 69-73 of his book *A Tour to Quebec, in the Autumn of 1819* (London, 1822). The use of four dots in the first three instances, and in the fifth, indicates the omission only of subheadings in the text.

At the village of Longueuil, or a little before arriving there, we caught the first view of Montreal. The first impression of this city is very pleasing. In its turrets and steeples, glittering with tin; in its thickly-built streets, stretching between one and two miles along the river, and rising gently from it; in its environs, ornamented with country-houses and green fields; in the noble expanse of the St. Lawrence, sprinkled with islands; in its foaming and noisy rapids; and in the bold ridge of the mountain, which forms the back-ground of the city, we recognize all the features necessary to a rich and magnificent landscape, and perceive, among these indications, decisive proofs of a flourishing inland emporium. . . .

If we experienced some elevation of feeling at the first view of the St. Lawrence, we were not likely to have our pride cherished by the means which conveyed us over this mighty river. Two Canadian boatmen ferried us over in a canoe, hollowed out of a single log. Our baggage being duly placed, we were desired to sit, face to face, on some clean straw placed on boards, which lay across the bottom of the boat: we were situated thus low, that our weight might not disturb the balance of the canoe, and we were requested to sit perfectly still. Our passage was to be nearly three miles obliquely up stream, and a part of the way against some powerful rapids.

Between us and Montreal, considerably up the stream, lay the brilliant island of St. Helena. It is elevated, commands a fine view of the city, is strongly marked by entrenchments, is fertile, and covered in part with fine timber. It is a domain, and we were much struck with the beautiful situation of the house on the south side of the island, belonging to the Baroness Lonqueil [Longueuil]. With the island and river it would form a fine subject for a picture.

Our boatmen conveyed us, without much difficulty, to

the southern point of this island, between which and the city, owing to the compression of the river by the island, a powerful rapid rushes along with much agitation, and a current which it is very difficult to stem. At the point of the island, particularly a branch of the river, confined by rocks, dashes along, almost with the rapidity of water bursting from a flood-gate, Through this strait it was necessary to pass, and, for some time, the boat went back, and even after landing us on the island, the canoe was coming around broadside to the current, when we were apprehensive that our baggage must be thrown into the river; but, by main strength, they pushed the boat through this torrent, and along the shore of the island, till the rapid became so moderate, that they ventured again to take us in, and push for the city. It took these poor fellows a toilsome hour to convey us over, and they demanded but a pittance for their services. . . .

We mounted a steep slippery bank, from the river, and found ourselves in one of the principal streets of the city. It required no powerful effort of the imagination to conceive that we were arrived in Europe. A town, compactly built of stone, without wood or brick, indicating permanency, and even a degree of antiquity, presenting some handsome public and private buildings, an active and numerous population, saluting the ear with two languages, but principally with the French — every thing seems foreign, and we easily feel that we are a great way from home. . . .

We were no sooner ushered into the mansion-house, a vast building, constructed of hewn stone, than we could easily imagine ourselves in one of the principal coffee-houses of London. Assiduity, kindness, quiet, and, in a word, domestic comfort, in every particular, except the absence of the family circle, were at once in our possession. . . .

The weather being mild and fine, parlour-fires were not yet kindled in Canada, but, as we preferred a fire for ourselves, we retired at candle lighting into a large and well-furnished room, with a bow end, and overlooking a terrace, thirty feet wide and one hundred and forty-four long, which is the length of the house. This terrace is thirty feet above the river, immediately on its brink, and commands a view of it, for many miles up and down the stream, and of the country on the other shore, thus presenting a most delightful prospect. This room was our parlour, while we remained in the house, and we were particularly fond of viewing from its windows, and from the terrace below, the fine scenes of twilight and evening on the St. Lawrence.

We had anticipated some inconvenience in visiting Canada so late in the season, on account of the shortness of the days; but the long and bright twilight, both at morning and evening, made us ample amends, and we found as much light as we left behind us, although less of sunshine. At half-after five, with the sun down, and the moon at the full, in the firmament, we sit at the dinner-table, apparently in broad day-light.

From the moment the sun is down, every thing becomes silent on the shore, which our windows overlook, and the murmurs of the broad St. Lawrence, more than two miles wide, immediately before us, and a little way to the right, spreading to five or six miles in breadth, are sometimes for an hour the only sounds that arrest our attention. Every evening since we have been here, black clouds and splendid moonlight have hung over and embellished this tranquil scene; and on two of those evenings we have been attracted to the window, by the plaintive Canadian boat-song. In one instance, it arose from a solitary voyager, floating in his light canoe, which occasionally appeared and disappeared on the sparkling river; and in its distant course seemed no larger than some sporting insect. In another instance a larger boat, with more numerous and less melodious voices, not indeed in perfect harmony, passed nearer to the shore, and gave additional life to the scene. A few moments after the moon broke out from a throne of dark clouds, and seemed to convert the whole expanse of water into one vast sheet of glittering silver, and in the very brightest spot, at the distance of more than a mile, again appeared a solitary boat, but too distant to admit of our hearing the song, with which the boatman was probably solacing his lonely course. . . .

The mere contemplation of a river, presenting such a broad expanse of water, at the distance of five hundred miles from the ocean, is interesting and pleasing. At this season it is a tranquil scene, but the river presents very considerable diversity. On our right it spreads into a broad lake, generally smooth, but in numbers of places it is ruffled by rapids and broken by ledges of rocks; on the left it runs with great rapidity, between the island of St. Helena and the city, and presents at all times a lively and magnificent water-course.

Occasionally, sloops, ships, and steam-boats are seen on the river, either passing rapidly down, or struggling against the current, but the most common craft of the river is of every size, from a small canoe to the largest boats that are built, without decks.

The margin of the river adjoining the city is, at most places where there are no wharfs, lined with floating-rafts and separate logs, intended both for fuel and for timber.

A scene of considerable activity is exhibited immediately before our terrace, by the carts and horses which are driven into the river, as far as is necessary, and frequently till the horses can hardly keep their feet; the object is to obtain the wood, which is thus conveniently loaded, as the body of the cart is as low as the surface of the river; and single sticks, too large for the carts, are drawn out separately by the horses. The carts are also used for the conveyance of water-casks to supply the city; the horses are driven into the water, and the casks are filled, very conveniently, without removing them from the cart.

We frequently observed on the Sorel river the French women washing at the river's edge. The same employment is seen here before our windows. Sometimes the clothes are placed on boards, in the river, and pounded; and at other times, the women dance on them, dashing the water about like ducks, and seemingly as much for frolic as for work. All these employments are attended with much vociferation, and contribute to give life and interest to the quiet scenes of a great inland water.

Some of the circumstances which I have just mentioned are, it is true, trivial, but still they tend to characterise the country and its inhabitants.

Though the *voyageurs* were once part of the Montreal scene, they really did not belong to the city, any more than they belonged to the villages and farms. The restless life of the rivers and lakes had claimed them. For all its hardships, they would have found any other way of life dull and tame.

Thomas Storrow Brown had seen them on the Montreal waterfront at the end of April, before they set out for the North-west. Even there they seemed to keep to themselves, gathering in the Old Market (now Place Royale), where they spent a few days drinking and fighting, "nobody interfering in it, as it was all among themselves and good natured, for even the fighting was without ill will, only to give proofs of strength and endurance."

On the hardihood and skill of the *voyageurs* the whole fur trade from Montreal depended. And it was a dangerous livelihood. Daniel Harmon, who set out from Lachine to serve as a clerk at a post of the North West Company, wrote of the rapids of the Ottawa, when he had reached Roche Capitaine Portage: "During the day, we have come up several difficult ones, where many persons have been drowned, either in coming up or going down. For every such unfortunate person, whether his corpse is found or not, a cross is erected by his companions, agreeably to a custom of the Roman Catholics; and at this place, I see no less than fourteen."

The description of setting out with the *voyageurs*, written about 1819 by the English scientist, Dr. John Jeremiah Bigsby, is remarkable for its realism. The *voyageurs*, for all their courage and hardihood, did not have the appearance of romantic figures; they were "a motley set to the eye," though all were picked men.

The great age of the *voyageurs* in Montreal ended when the North West Company was merged with the Hudson's Bay Company in 1821, and the more economical route through Hudson Bay was preferred. Sir George Simpson, Governor of the Hudson's Bay Company, kept up his departures with the *voyageurs* from Lachine, but more from a picturesque personal taste, than for any economic reason. The Montreal era of the *voyageurs* of the canoes may be said to have come to an end with his death in 1860.

This excerpt is from Dr. Bigsby's book *The Shoe and Canoe* . . . (London, 1850), volume I, pages 126-7, 129-35. A footnote on page 126 has been omitted. The "Chateau-brillant" to which he refers is the old ruined fort still standing in Senneville.

At length the day of departure, the 20th of May,

arrived. Together with a pleasant young clerk of the North-west Company I left Montreal in a long-eared calash, drawn by two stout black horses, for the mouth of the river Ottawa, at the upper end of the Island of Montreal — there to embark in the light canoe.

The main business of the canoe in which I was granted a seat was to convey Mr. Rocheblave, a partner in the North-west Company, and his clerk, to Fort William, in Lake Superior; and M. Tabeau, a Roman Catholic priest, and myself, to the Straits of St. Mary, the outlet of the above lake, and my furthest point on this occasion. . . .

We jogged on . . . past St. Anne's, celebrated by the poet, to Château-brillant, a small fort, venerable in ruins, overlooking from a mound the Narrows at the mouth of the Ottawa. It is overgrown with ivy and young trees, and was once meant to overawe the neighbouring Indians. . . .

Our *voyageurs* were to have awaited us at Château-brillant; but, save for our own shouts, all was still among its shadows. Returning a couple of miles, we found them at Forbes' Tavern . . .

I was now introduced to our leader, M. Rocheblave, a senior partner of the North-west Company, a tall dark Frenchman, with a stoop, born at New Orleans. I found him well informed, obliging, and companionable. He would have been more so during the first few days of our voyage, but he had been only *very* recently married.

Let me not forget M. Tabeau, the curé of Boucherville, a stout, rosy, happy-looking priest of middle age, of unaffected and even polished manners, fond of music, and reasonably so of good living. He was (and I hope still lives) a good man, and had nothing of the livid complexion and gloomy pugnacity of many of the Roman Catholic clergy in England.

I have already mentioned Mr. Robinson, the clerk. At once I felt that I was fortunate in my companions, and took my seat in the canoe at Forbes' Tavern, not a little excited by my new position, and by the romance (to me at least) of ascending almost to the source of the lovely and beautiful Ottawa. . . .

Our canoe was thirty-six feet long, sharp at each end, six feet wide in the middle, and made of birch bark, in sheets sewn together with vegetable fibre, and the seams gummed up close. The sides are strengthened and steadied by four or six cross-bars lashed to the rim of the canoe, and the inside is protected by slender ribs of a light wood, but the bottom only by a few loose poles. It is called a light canoe, or "canot lâche," because intended to go swiftly, and to carry only provisions and personal baggage. Its usual complement is nineteen — that is, fifteen paddlemen and four gentlemen passengers; the latter sitting each on his rolled-up bed in the middle compartment.

The North-west Company provided *munitions de bouche* on the most liberal scale — port, madeira, shrub, brandy, rum, sausages, eggs, a huge pie of veal and pheasants, cold roast beef, salt beef, hams, tongues, loaves, tea, sugar, and, to crown all, some exquisite beaver tail. The men were provided well in a plainer way, and had their glass of rum in cold and rainy weather.

I was disappointed and not a little surprised at the appearance of the *voyageurs*. On Sundays, as they stand round the door of the village churches, they are proud dressy fellows in their parti-coloured sashes and ostrich-feathers; but here they were a motley set to the eye: but the truth was that all of them were picked men, with extra wages as serving in a light canoe.

Some were well made, but all looked weak in the legs, and were of light weight. A Falstaff would have put his foot through the canoe to the "yellow sands" beneath. The collection of faces among them chanced to be extraordinary, as they squatted, paddle in hand, in two rows, each on his slender bag of necessaries. By the bye, all their finery (and they love it) was left at home. One man's face, with a large Jewish nose, seemed to have been squeezed in a vice, or to have passed through a flattening machine. It was like a cheese-cutter — all edge. Another had one nostril bitten off. He proved the buffoon of the party. He had the extraordinary faculty of untying the strings of his face, as it were, at pleasure, when his features fell into confusion — into a crazed chaos almost frightful; his eye, too, lost its usual significance: but no man's countenance (barring the bite) was fuller of fun and fancies than his, when he liked. A third man had his features wrenched to the right — exceedingly little, it is true; but the effect was remarkable. He had been slapped on the face by a grisly bear. Another was a short, paunchy old man, with vast features, but no forehead — the last man I should have selected; but he was a hard-working creature, usually called "Passe-partout," because he had been everywhere, and was famous for the weight of fish he could devour at a meal. He knew the flavour of the fish of each great lake, just as the man who had been ordered by Boerhaave to live on broth made of grass came to know the field from whence it was taken. Except the younger men, their faces were short, thin, quick in their expression, and mapped out in furrows, like those of the sunday-less Parisians. Nothing could exceed their respectful and obliging behaviour. The same must be said of all of this class with whom I had anything to do. . . . Our worthy priest, M. Tabeau, while on shore, shook every *voyageur* by the hand kindly, and had a pleasant word for each. We then embarked at thirty minutes past three P.M.

As soon as we were well settled down in our places, and the canoe began to feel the paddles, Mr. Tabeau, by way of asking a blessing on the voyage, pulled off his hat, and sounded forth a Latin invocation to the Deity, and to a long train of male and female saints, in a loud and full voice, while all the men, at the end of each versicle, made response, *"Qu'il me bénisse."*

This done, he called for a song; and many were gleefully carolled — each verse in solo, and then repeated in chorus, north-west fashion. Of such use is singing, in enabling the men to work eighteen and nineteen hours a-day (at a pinch), through forests and across great bays, that a good singer has additional pay. The songs are sung with might and main, at the top of the voice, timed to the paddle, which makes about fifty strokes in a minute. While nearing habitations, crossing sheets of water, and during rain, the song is loud and long. The airs I suppose to be ancient French. They are often very beautiful.

3

Rigours and Recreations, 1830-1840

Almost from the first, and certainly till the last, the nineteenth century saw a tide of immigrants flowing through Montreal for the West, though the "West," of course, was an expanding term, a frontier always new and farther away. This vast movement of people, with all their expectations and problems, provided a spectacle for the thoughtful observer. It was a spectacle touching or laughable, courageous or tawdry, according to the eye of the beholder.

An unsentimental view of the immigrants was taken by an anonymous writer about the year 1820. He saw them setting out for the West from Lachine, noisy, disorderly and dirty. At that time, before the opening of the Lachine Canal (and often afterwards), immigrants had to make their way overland from Montreal, with all their belongings, the nine miles to Lachine on Lake St. Louis. There they went aboard one of the bateaux — the huge flat-bottomed boats which were propelled up the St. Lawrence by oars, sails, ropes and poles. The bateaux, about thirty feet long, and heavily built to withstand the blows and strains of the river, carried great weights; passengers and baggage were crowded into them. Usually there was no protection against the weather, except, perhaps, an awning.

This anonymous writer, calling himself "The Itinerant,"

had a mind free from the anxious preoccupations of the immigrants. He was travelling only for travel's sake; "for I like to 'keep moving'," he said. He suggested the scene "would defy the ever varying pencil of a Hogarth to pourtray." And his own picture is in the Hogarthian spirit.

This description of the immigrants leaving Lachine, though apparently written about 1820, appeared in *The Canadian Magazine or Literary Repository*, March, 1824 and April, 1824.

The wharf, alongside of which was the boat, presented a heterogeneous mixture of bedding, baggage, trunks, men women, and children, all laid in one heterogeneous heap. The crew and male passengers were busily enjoyed in tumbling this promiscuous group into the boat. . . .

The Captain a civil polite man, apparently about 50 years of age, was conspicuous for nothing so much as his indefatigable attention to make his passengers as comfortable as he could. He had been, as I afterwards learned, employed in this forwarding trade for some years; and had from his intercourse with various persons passing that way, acquired that most useful of all knowledge, the art of pleasing every one. To his superiors whom he could recognise in a moment, he was polite and respectful, with his equals in rank or even inferiors he could indulge in a jest without vulgar familiarity. His crew may be described *en masse* as a set of ugly, shabby looking fellows, in their apparel. . . . Another division of the party attracted my notice. It consisted of the husband, wife and four young children, all plentifully imbued with dirt. They seemed all in a bustle and hurry without doing any one thing to accelerate the embarkation of their luggage; and in such a degree of confusion as to be ignorant which article they should first take hold of. In the midst of this hubbub — the husband exclaimed: "sure Mary, and y'eve forgotten the little box wi' the childers duds." "Och Dennis an it's me that has. Run back jewel an fetch it." "Captain, honey, will ye wait for him?" "Where is it?" said the Captain, "he must be quick, I'll be off in ten minutes." The application to the Captain, if not a bull, was certainly a blunder, the unfortunate "childers duds" had been left in Montreal, six or seven miles off, and must there wait for another opportunity. The bewailing of this omission (no doubt serious to those who made it) rendered them utterly unable to put the remainder of their luggage on board. The poor mother sat down and vented her sorrow in piteous ejaculations, while the father standing mute and seemingly overcome with the disappointment, was hustled unresistingly on board among the crowd. There were two Scotch families (numbers uncounted) which sustained their part in the scene. While the males were standing together in close conversation with their hands in the pockets of their small clothes; the females (a peculiarity I have before witnessed) were allowed to bear the labouring oar. They were tugging and pulling at their heavy chests and bundles, while their unfeeling mates, stood with their faculties engrossed in the all powerful propensity of staring.... "John," exclaimed one of the females, "y'eve forgot the keys, I'll wager." "Na, I hae them in my pouch," replied the husband, and turning away relapsed into his quondam indifference.... "Tak up the bairn," said the other female to her husband, "he'll tumble o'er the bank." "Come here, Tammie," said the father, "come to me my wee callant, ye manna gang there;" at the same time accompanying his request by a motion towards the child, a nice chubby boy about three years of age, and who clearly shewed parental mandates had little effect upon him unless accordant with his own will. The little fellow when seized screamed and struggled violently, and in the bustle off went his hat into the river. This event produced a hubbub and stir among the spectators, nearly as great as if the head had accompanied the hat. It was soon fished up however and replaced upon the curly pate of the little urchin, who received it with surly indifference, and could not, either by promise of reward, or threat of future punishment, be prevailed upon to thank the boatman who had rescued it. . . . After a little time we were all safely embarked, without any loss or damage, except the shoe of one of the children, which had dropt into the river, and *heu me miserum*, sunk to rise no more, at the moment the father was handing him from the wharf into the outstretched arms of his mother on board the batteaux. I got on board, and seated myself in the most conspicuous part of the boat . . .

The hurried and impatient glances cast by the Captain towards the inn fronting the wharf, and the accompanying movement of pulling out and putting up his watch, led to the suspicion that something was expected from that quarter. And while I was ruminating where we should "stow away" any thing farther, for the boat was deep loaded, and overtopped with heaps on heaps of baggage piled high above the gunwales, my doubts were solved. For on turning my eye up the wharf, I observed another detachment moving in the direction of the boat. At the head of it, and well befitting the station, came a genteel looking, middle aged gentleman, dressed in the usual travelling equipment — a blue surtout — dark pantaloons and boots; with a female, of an elegant figure, leaning on his arm. — The rear was brought up by two men carrying

a large trunk between them, and their other hands occupied the one with a travelling bag — the other with a birds'
cage containing a pair of canaries. So that the whole of the
live part of our cargo, with the exception of such as belonged to the insect or vermes tribe was composed of the
biped class. The air and gesture of this new comer, showed
"he had seen the world" as the phrase is. His military
address pointed him out in a moment as a son of Mars,
while the unremitted and respectful attention he bestowed
upon his female companion, indicated his devotions were
not exclusively confined to the god of war. On a nearer
approach, his sun-burnt, but still handsome manly face,
exhibited the rough usage of many a foreign clime; and
from this I (and as I afterwards found justly) concluded
he had seen service.

Having got this last party on board; and the cabin
passengers (if I may use the term) being all adjusted in
their places, the scene shifted and a new part of the performance was commenced. The boatmen having by dint
of pushing, packing, squeezing and rolling the animate
and inanimate parts of the cargo, got fairly seated at the
oars; we pushed off and in seaman's phrase got fairly afloat.
We now moved slowly foreward under the propulsive
efforts of the boatmen, in one of the sweetest evenings, and
in sight of one of the most beautiful prospects, the heated
mind of a mahometan could ever depict in painting his
celestial paradise. . . .

All are slaves to the wish of appearing to advantage;
and in spite of the beauty of the surrounding scenery, the
pleasantness of the evening and the engaging attractions
of the group of which I formed a part, the first thought
which occupied my mind, was, what would be our appear-

ance when viewed from the shore. In the forepart of the boat was a motly mass of male and female, old and young heads — peeping over the gunwale; which in their ill adorned and uncombed state, combined with the tattered dirty dresses, formed a picture which would defy the ever varying pencil of a Hogarth to pourtray. The bundles of baggage piled heaps on heaps, seen at a distance, intersected the line of the horison like a haystack; but on a nearer view seemed like a rocky mountain in miniature. Seated among this chaos-like heap of ruins the rowers were seen pursuing their see-saw vocation with steady regularity. The rest of the group seated under the awning in the stern, differed in the appearance of their dresses, and had an aspect approaching to what might be termed cabin passengers. . . .

The fast declining sun now gave an encreased beauty to the landscape. Every person has witnessed this effect in a summer's evening; and many writers have described it — glowing colours — rich tints — sombre hue and mellowness, with a thousand other tropes metaphors and figures, have been put in requisition to describe the picture, and convey to the mind by words what every eye can have an opportunity of beholding. I shall not waste time on the subject. It is sufficient to say the change produced its full effect upon all of us. The firey fumes of the spirits which at our out-set had operated in noisy mirth on the boatmen, were dissipated by their exertions at the oars; and they now silently plied their weary tasks, striving to reach the end of their day's journey. The approach of the evening had an additional effect upon the present party and different from what I had ever before seen. The tranquillity of the scene produced a corresponding quietness in the be-holders, as is always the case. The squaling and caterwaling of the children in the bow of the boat, became more and more faint as the sun descended. It had been incessant during the afternoon — and required all our stentorian power to enable each other to be heard: but at last the drowsy god accomplished what had defied the scoldings, threats, promises and beatings from the mothers, and laid the little imps in calm repose under his oblivious veil, and left those, so inclined, to enjoy the full pleasure of a contemplative mood.

Through most of the nineteenth century — certainly through its first three-quarters — New Year's was a greater occasion for merry-making than Christmas. Christmas was the religious holiday, celebrated by the French Canadians with midnight Mass — a service that always drew a certain number of Protestants as respectful onlookers. But New Year's was the great season of visiting.

At New Year's visits had to be made to all relations, friends and leading personages in the community. The custom was also Scottish, and as the English-speaking people of the city were largely Scots, the traditions blended, each confirming the other. These were not traditions favourable to temperance, as hospitality was offered to every visitor, but they were generally regarded as favourable to good feeling. Friendships were kept in repair, and even those who had quarrelled during the year could be reconciled by New Year's visits, when everyone was made welcome.

A lively description of Christmas and New Year's in Montreal in the 1820's was written, as memories, by an anonymous contributor to *The New Dominion Monthly,* Montreal, in an article headed "The Holidays Forty Years Ago," in the issue for January, 1868. He describes the drive in the little sleighs — the "carioles" — for midnight Mass at Pointe aux Trembles, and the New Year's visits, when the streets "were, of course, like a fair with visitors coming and going in all directions."

On Christmas-eve, in the year 182—, a number of young

men of Montreal hired two or three *Marche-doncs*, to go down to the *Messe de Minuit*, or Midnight Mass, at Pointe aux Trembles, then a favorite sleigh ride. One of the party had arrived that fall from the "Old Country," or "Home," as Britain was affectionately called, and the others were bent on showing him the wonders of this French country, with which a residence of some years had made them familiar. The *Marche-donc* was the common name for the small but comfortable cariole of those days, usually pronounced by old-country people, "carry-all;" but the pronunciation was inappropriate, for, so far from carrying all of a party, it would only carry two passengers comfortably in the low, wide seat behind, though, in case of need, a third might sit on the high, narrow seat in front with the *"charretier,"* or driver. These carioles were well provided with straw in the bottom, and buffalo robes; and the greatcoats, muffling-shawls, and huge fur caps with ears, usually worn in those days, rendered the upper part of the body safe from even the cold of a Canadian mid-winter night. The *charretiers* were smart, attentive French-Canadians, and their horses, being of the pure Canadian breed, were very fast and long-winded. Indeed, a hardier or more serviceable race of horses could not be found for a climate like that of Canada . . .

The low cariole was so very comfortable that many regretted the necessity, imposed by law some time after, of using high runners, and, as soon as that law was repealed, not a few returned to the old fashion. Indeed, you will now see the most fashionable turnouts in the city of Montreal in the shape of the old-fashioned cariole, or Berlin — only a little lower and smaller. The fare for these vehicles was so low that clerks on very moderate salaries could afford an occasional drive, and very healthy and pleasant those drives were, if they did not lead, as was too often the case, to drinking in some country tavern.

The party already introduced to the reader "embarked" — as the phrase was and is among French-Canadians — in their carioles at the Place d'Armes, a queer, old-fashioned square. . . .

Our young men embarked, then, on the night in question, at the Place d'Armes, and the horses — tired, doubtless, of standing for hours in the cold, — trotted away along Notre Dame street at a rate that would have delighted even Jerome, of Jerome Park, or Bonner, of the New York *Ledger.* . . .

Dashing away past Handyside's distillery — now in ruins — the party passed the Cross — so-called, though there was no cross there — and continued along the open road to Longue Pointe. Here was another distillery of the Handysides, — now, also, in ruins, — with the little creek winding past it, at the *embouchure* of which Jacques Cartier probably landed when he marched through the woods to visit the Indian village of Hochelaga, somewhere near McGill College Avenue. No other object of special interest was seen in this moonlight journey until the party reached Pointe aux Trembles, where, after warming themselves at the stove of the village tavern, they made their way to the Church. The altar was decorated with evergreens and artificial flowers, and there was a "dim religious light" produced by wax candles. Soon the mass commenced, the church being well filled by the parishioners and visitors from the city. After mass, which had nothing particularly striking in its celebration, the youths "embarked" in their carioles again and hurried homewards, bidding each other good-bye till New Year's day, which they agreed to spend together in making New Year's visits. ... And now for the great holiday of the year. ...

About eleven o'clock on New Year's day, 182—, the young men who had attended midnight mass at Pointe aux Trembles, on Christmas-eve, met according to appointment at the lodgings of one of their number, and sallied forth for a day's visiting. It was the custom then — and is still, to some extent — to go in companies of three, four, or five, to perform this pleasing duty, and it was the privilege of all to visit at every house where any one of the company had even the most casual acquaintance. Indeed, this was sometimes dispensed with, and a company of visitors, availing themselves of the privilege of the day, would go boldly into houses where none of them had any acquaintance, especially if those houses contained attractive young ladies. This was a hazardous experiment, but we never heard of any case in which the impertinence was resented. The ladies of the house — then as now — were arrayed in their best apparel, and received and returned the New Year's salutations of visitors with affability and grace. But there was one important difference in those salutations. An old French custom had come down, almost unimpaired, to the time of which we write, though it has fallen into disuse since, except among relations. This custom consisted in the visitors kissing the ladies, a privilege confined exclusively to New Year's visits. There was another custom universal then, which has since been greatly and very beneficially modified. Every house had wines and liquors on a side-table, with a tray of cakes, and every visitor was by usage compelled to drink to the health of the ladies. The sense of hospitality would have been shocked with any omission of this custom — now so happily superseded by coffee instead of liquors in very many families, and in all cases by entire freedom to partake of refreshments or not, as the visitor sees fit. The number of visits paid and received at the New Year was a matter of pride and a subject of conversation. Of course, when a long list of visits had to be got through in a day, they were short; in fact a fashionable house had a continual stream of comers and goers, from eleven or twelve o'clock in the forenoon, till five or even half-past five in the afternoon. Gentlemen, of course, visited most in their own circle of acquaintance, but they were bound to visit all their friends and acquaintances, poor relations and dependents included. Every one, also, was expected to visit his minister or priest, who remained at home on that day, and repaid the visits the next week. Though New Year's-day was the great day for visiting, yet it was construed to last for the remainder of the week, and visits were often continued for two or three days, though the number of visitors rapidly decreased. They could not, however, be run into the next week, that being devoted, as we have said before, to return-calls of ministers and priests. By this custom of visiting, acquaintanceships were kept up, and families between whom any coldness or dryness had occurred could with propriety renew their friendship by a New Year's visit. The streets were, of course, like a fair with visitors coming and going in all directions, on foot, or in sleighs and carioles, and good-humor was universal.

Throughout New Year's-day, sleighs loaded with youths, some of them with noisy musical instruments, and others singing and shouting, went round the streets of the city.

After a hard day's work, in which our party paid fifty or more visits, they retired to their cheerless boarding-houses, sighing at the thought that they had not yet homes of their own.

Harrison Stephens was an outstanding example of the Yankee trader in Montreal — shrewd, enterprising, self-reliant, persevering, difficult at times and strong-willed. Born in Jamaica, Vermont, in 1801, of old New England stock, he set up in business for the first time at the age of seventeen, when he made a contract to build a portion of the Whitehall Canal. He then went into storekeeping, operated a tannery, and first moved over the border when he established a factory in the Eastern Townships.

Stephens came to Montreal in 1828, and began importing goods from New York. He turned his hand to nearly every kind of trade and finance and prospered so well that in 1845, when only forty-four, he is said to have retired to spend "the rest of his life . . . enjoying the laurels of his well earned patrimony." His retirement was largely nominal, for he remained active in business, but by 1845 he had made his fortune.

In Montreal he kept his American pride, serving as consul of the United States, and flying the Stars and Stripes in the grounds of his mansion on Dorchester Street (immediately west of the St. James's Club). He named his son George Washington Stephens — a name that was passed on to his grandson.

In his old age he described business conditions as he had known them in Montreal in his early years, and how he matched his wits against monopoly and authority. His description of taking two tons of silver to New York by sleigh in winter, riding the sleigh himself, was not altogether peculiar. The first accountant of the Bank of Montreal, H. Dupuy, has described how he brought two tons of specie in boxes from the Kingston branch to Montreal in the ordinary stage, with no one to guard the money but himself and the driver. Though Harrison Stephens had his dispute with the Bank of Montreal, the subsequent reconciliation was very complete indeed, for he was a director of the bank from 1845 to 1857.

These recollections by Harrison Stephens have the notation "as taken from his dictation," which would explain their informal manner and occasional repetitions. A transcript of the dictation was preserved by the family, and this excerpt is reproduced from the copy in the possession of Mr. Murray Ballantyne of Montreal. (The Customs House Square to which Stephens refers is now known as Place Royale.)

I arrived in Montreal in the year 1828, and started business as an importer of American goods from New York. I commenced principally with rice and tobacco. At that time the Americans were in bad repute owing to the fact that there was no extradition treaty between Canada and the United States, and everybody who had committed a crime in the States fled the country and took protection in Canada, which, of course, gave a very bad odour to the American name here. The population of Montreal at that time I think would be about twenty-five thousand. There were no macadamised roads, the present wharves were not built, and ships came right up alongside into the mud. There was still in those days a portion of the old fortifications standing which is now covered by the site of the present Montreal House, in Custom House Square. Custom House Square was then a market place, and was the principal place of business, the principal trade was done there. In those days there was a gate there into the city, and if a man wanted to sell a hundred bags of flour he would go and stand there at the gateway of the fortification. . . . The Old Countryman's Inn, with its wooden galleries, situated on the corner of St. Sulpice Street, was one of the principal hotels at that time. There was no Merchants Exchange then, and in fact the business was chiefly transacted at what was called the old market, where the Custom House Square now is. The North-West Company

and the Hudson [Hudson's] Bay Company were the headquarters of everything — a Mr. Thaine was the factor then.
The tea trade was monopolized by the East India Company, who were the only parties allowed to sell it at that
time. They sold periodically at upset prices at auction, no
bid less than a penny was taken, and deposit of $10 for
every chest that was struck down to you or you would not
get it. The East India Company was represented here by
Forsyth, Richardson & Co., until the Company was abol-
ished. No private individual could import tea, and the
only way you could get it was either from the East India
Company, or to buy it in New York and smuggle it into
Canada. There was a great deal of smuggling in those
days — principally in tea and tobacco. Ben Davis was a fair
specimen of a smuggler at that time — and I did a little
at it myself; I did not go into it very heavily because of
the risk, but it was not a very great risk because it was so
popular then. . . .

When I first came to the city the population consisted
of about two-thirds French, there were a few English and
still fewer Irish. The trade was concentrated in the hands
of the East India Company; there were a few private
traders, the trade being confined to a few large houses.
The principal export of the country at that time was
wheat, which was for the most part raised in Lower Canada — in the Chambly and Richelieu districts principally
— and sold at three shillings a bushel in the States. The
only Bank then was the Bank of Montreal until the City
Bank was incorporated. The Bank of Montreal would not
discount a dollar for me in the year 1830. At that time the
Hon. Peter McGill was President of the Bank, and Benjamin Holmes was Cashier. After having kept an account

with them for a long time, and a respectable line of deposit, I was positively refused by the Cashier, Mr. Holmes, a discount of very choice paper, stating that it would be unnecessary for me to make any application of that character, because I would meet with no prospect of success. From that time I drew payments in specie for large amounts, as I wanted to remit to New York. Soon afterwards I drew upwards of $154,000 in silver, which I carried to New York in winter, riding on the sleigh myself. For this amount of silver I required two double teams, as I took as much as two tons of silver with me, depositing it in New York and drawing my drafts against it. I made a profit on that transaction of two per cent, and I continued that policy until the Bank came to terms with me. Mr. John Torrance came to me in regard to the matter on behalf of the Bank, stating that it was injurious to the whole trade of the country, and to my own interests, and that I would, in company with them, ultimately suffer by it. He asked me to resume my business with the Bank, and leave all questions of drawing specie out of the question. I told him as he was a great friend of mine, and as he desired it and asked it as a personal favour, I would certainly do it; and from that time my business connections with the Bank have been very satisfactory.

The name "Priests' Farm," still applied to the stretch of land above Sherbrooke Street, west of Côte des Neiges, is a reminder of the days when the Gentlemen of St. Sulpice had their farm in this area. Their headquarters on this farm — their manor-house — was at the old fort, whose two round front towers may still be seen over the wall of the Grand Séminaire, at the head of Fort Street.

The fort had been built at the end of the seventeenth century to protect their mission to the Iroquois, who were settled on the fields nearby. When the Iroquois were moved to a new site at Sault-au-Récollet in the sixteen-nineties, the old fort — known as "Fort des Messieurs" — became the country residence of the Sulpicians.

The "Priests' Farm" was used for summer holidays both by the Sulpicians and by the boys they taught in the Collège de Montréal (known as the "Petit Séminaire") on College Street, a little to the west of McGill Street. The boys of the "Petit Séminaire" have been described, dressed in their long blue coats with parti-coloured sashes, and headed by their band, marching from College Street to the Priests' Farm for a holiday in the country.

When the new Governor-in-Chief of Canada, Lord Aylmer, came to Montreal for the first time, in 1831, he, with Lady Aylmer and their party, drove out from the Government House (the Château de Ramezay) on Notre Dame Street to visit the Sulpicians at the Priests' Farm, "about two miles from Montreal." It was a suitable day for such a visit, as Montreal was suffering "Calcutta heat," and at the Priests' Farm the June breeze could be felt even indoors.

Lady Aylmer wrote her account of the visit (with inconsistency of spelling and punctuation) in the notes and extracts from letters which she gathered as a manuscript and headed "Recollections of Canada: 1831." It was printed in *Rapport de l'Archiviste de la Province de Québec pour 1934-35* (Quebec, 1935). This selection will be found on pages 308-9.

As we have been some time now settled in Montreal, my young nieces may Expect some little account of this Town and its Environs ... The last week we have been at several Fetes given to us on our arrival at Montreal, and as it is rather unusual to hear of Priests of the Catholic Religion giving Entertainments to Heretics like ourselves, it may amuse you to hear an account of these fêtes. As the strictness of their habits does not admit of the Superior or Brother's of the Seminary giving invitations, in order to gratify them, and meet this difficulty, it was arranged that the Governor was to Express his intention of Visiting the

Establishment and I was to say that it would be agreeable to me to accompany him. This point of Etiquette agreed on, I was to invite any Ladies I liked to accompany me, and I accordingly selected those whom I thought it would be most agreeable to the party to receive, taking care to have Canadians and Catholics in preference. The party invited met at our house at half past Eleven, the time appointed, and we all drove in open carriages to the Priests farm about two miles from Montreal under the hill, called here "the Mountain" and from which Montreal takes its present name. . . . The Priests' farm is a very beautifully situated country house to which these poor men have the comfort of going as a *Relache* once a week and where they have some good rooms plainly furnished; among other luxuries shade and a Billiard Table. Here they spend one day in every week and the youth who are Educating at the Seminary go out early in the morning twice a week and dine and spend the day in such amusements as boys generally prefer. We were received at the Portico of the house by Monsr Quibleiy [Quiblier], the Superior with whom we had previously made acquaintance by his having dined with Lord Aylmer, and his having Visited me twice. He is a very agreable intelligent man, and would be a favorite in any society, as there is a kindliness and benevolence in his manners very prepossessing. The Bishop of Telmesse was invited to meet us, and as he is styled *Monseigneur* (though not an acknowledged Bishop, by the Government) he takes precedency in courtesy. I was conducted by the *Directeur du Séminaire,* Monsr Quiblier, to the Billiard Room, where the Ladies all seated themselves, the weather was Excessively hot so that our finding all the rooms well shaded and with a through draft, through, was a great luxury. We were soon summoned to the Collation prepared in the Refectory where among other ornaments one shone conspicuous being a Variety of small Silk Flags, with "Vittoria" "Talavera" "Fuentes d'Ono (ro)" &c, &c, all the actions in Spain, Portugal or elsewhere, in which the Governor had been, were displayed in compliment to him on various Elevated Mounds of Pastry in the form of Tower's, Trophies, &c, &c, on the cakes, and principle flag, the Armorial bearings &c, &c, were very well painted, and the whole being kept in gentle motion by the through air from the open Windows, produced a very pretty effect, and rendered our sitting at rather a substantial breakfast, not at all as unpleasant as the *gêne* of a hot room would have made it. The whole of the Brother's of the Seminary were, I believe, assembled on this occasion. I had invited Colonel Macintosh of the 15th and the Major and his family, so we were a mixture of Military and Clergy, Laity, &c, on this occasion, where all seemed to Vie with each other to display good fellowship, and I thought the Wine and good cheer did not seem disagreeable to any of the party there assembled. When the repast was over we walked towards the building where the students were all collected waiting our arrival and we placed ourselves under the trees, while one of the boys read an address prepared for the Governor which ended by a request for a holiday. This met, as you may imagine, with great applause, and I added my request for another so that our Visit was very agreable to the young ones, a very nice assemblage of boys of whom the superior seems very fond. Having had most of the Sons of the Gentlemen of Montreal and its Environs presented to us, we walked under the shade of some avenues which render this farm an agreeable resource for the Seminary, and then returned to the house where the carriages being driven up, we took leave...

Mrs. John Lovell's reminiscences of Montreal in the eighteen-thirties reveal the city as it appeared to the eyes of an active and perceptive girl. As a feminine view, it is all the more interesting for recapturing so many details of domestic life, from the family wash being taken in a cart down to the riverside at Pointe St. Charles to the way milk could be carried in a basket at Bonsecours Market and bacon hung in the brick-lined cellars. She also pictures the social life of the time: the sleigh-drives into the country, a visit to the military St. Helen's Island, and the old and young mingling happily at frequent small gatherings.

Mrs. Lovell was the daughter of a German merchant in Montreal, N. P. M. Kurczyn. The family house was on Notre Dame Street (in the western section then known as St. Joseph Street) near the head of St. Henry Street (the second street west of McGill). In 1849 she married John Lovell, one of the principal printers and publishers in Canada in the nineteenth century. He is said to have imported the first steam printing press into Canada, and from his printing plant issued a series of newspapers, magazines and books. His magazine *The Literary Garland* had such contributors as Mrs. Susanna Moody and Major John Richardson; among his books was such a triumph of colour printing as *Canadian Wild Flowers* by Mrs. Catherine Parr Traill and Agnes Fitzgibbon; and he aided Canadian business with his series of local and national directories. Mrs. Lovell shared her husband's literary tastes.

This selection is from Mrs. Lovell's book *Reminiscences of Seventy Years,* printed for private circulation in Montreal by John Lovell and Son, 1908, pages 1, 7-8, 13-15, 25-28, 35-36.

I intended to commence my reminiscences about 1837, the era of the Rebellion, but I recall incidents previous to that time. . . .

There were gardens and fields throughout what is now the city. My aunt's garden was on the east side of the Main

Street, near St. Catherine. There the delicious Fameuse apple was in perfection, also, the Bourassa, and Pommes Grises, apples that kept throughout the winter. A friend's garden was situated on Mountain Street below St. Catherine. Grapes were cultivated, and there were luscious strawberries. Our greengage and egg plums were far superior to those from California, for they had a richer flavour, when picked off the trees.

We had no cold storage, or refrigerators, but we had cellars, lined and paved with brick, well ventilated, where the winter fruit and vegetables were stored. There hung the home cured hams and bacon. On the shelves were ranged the bowls of milk with golden cream. The peas and beans tasted better in season, and the oranges, for which we waited patiently until June, were appreciated. Therefore, the present generation need not pride themselves on their superior advantages, for we had every comfort in those days.

There were no public conservatories that I remember, but a few private ones, among them one attached to the late Mr. Lunn's house, corner of DeBleury, now Park Avenue.

Most people cultivated their own flowers in the windows. My mother was very successful, and furnished me with a bouquet on occasions, for then we carried bouquet holders, and it was necessary to have them supplied. . . .

The city was not in a sanitary condition. Large barrels were kept at the doors in the yards, and the water was brought in barrels from the river.

My mother did not think the supply adequate for her laundry, so every Monday the clothes were taken to the river at Point St. Charles where there was a green plot, and where they could be bleached.

The preparation for this event caused great excitement in the kitchen. Tubs, wood, pots, and a well filled picnic basket had to be provided, and were taken in a large square cart which was called a "tombreaux."

Most people had their cows at that time. Our yard extended from St. Joseph to Bonaventure Street. I was often amused to see the boy go by with his horn to call them to pasture, and again in the evening bring them home. They would patiently wait until the gate was opened.

The Bonsecours Market was popular as it is now. It was scarcely believed in the Old Country, that milk could be carried in baskets. I saw this frequently. The milk was frozen in tureens, and then placed in a clean napkin and carried in a basket.

We saw many of the French Canadian habitants in heavy coat, tuque and moccasins, the women wearing quilted bonnets. What a jargon of voices as one passed through . . .

Chickens could be obtained for twenty-five cents a pair, and eggs at five pence a dozen.

We used only candles at that time. An occasional lamp was seen but supplied with olive oil. There was no kerosene.

The street lamps were fastened on posts. I often used to watch the men pass with ladder on shoulder, to light the lamps at dusk. . . .

I can recall . . . memories of Montreal in 1838-39. . . . Society in smaller circles where old and young mingled together, very much to the pleasure of both parties. Entertainments were less costly. There was an air of simplicity and true hospitality. We had a more steady prolonged winter. Our streets presented a lively appearance when the British troops were here. Several of the officers had handsome sleighs and beautiful horses. They invited ladies to accompany them on their drives. It was delightful to listen to the music of their well organized bands.

The Grenadiers with their high hats, and the Hussars on horseback with their picturesque dress, the jacket hanging from the shoulder. The reviews on the parade ground, the marching through the streets, all was stirring and interesting.

Notre Dame and St. James Streets were the favorite routes for the club drives, and handsome equipages were seen in winter with rich fur robes. . . .

For fuel we used nothing but wood. The special sleighs for conveying the wood had four posts on runners, the wood in large logs piled high. There were oblong stoves with three pipes called "gallows pipes" placed on top of the stove so as to throw out more heat. They became very hot in a few minutes but cooled off quickly. . . . The long pipes had to be shaken in February, and not infrequently they took fire, and then set the chimney on fire. . . .

Frequently through the winter we used to take long drives in the country. How delightful crossing the broad river, the ice sparkling in the sun. We would rest at intervals in some wayside inn, and better still visit friends whose hospitality was unbounded. It was interesting to visit some of the homes of the Canadian "habitants." How immaculately clean were the houses with their white-washed walls. The floors, tables and benches well polished. The cooking stove, a box one, with oven above. Oval and round mats on the floor made of strips of cotton dyed in various colors and woven with a native loom. Sacred pictures around. Bedsteads with patch-work quilts of many patterns. Three and four generations frequently were to be found in one house, for the "grand père" and "grand mère" were respected and kept their places by the hearth. Frugal, light of heart, these people were content, and imbued with deep religious feeling.

The sugaring parties must not be omitted. On one occasion I accompanied a party to Longue Pointe. The drive was delightful over the crisp snow, for the sunny days in March and frosty nights made the sap run. We found the syrup which had boiled for a long time ready to candy, and we poured some on the snow, when it became brittle at once. Then we made pancakes, and ate them with the fresh syrup.

We always returned refreshed and invigorated after those visits to the country. . . .

Not having any railways, the stage coach was regularly seen on our streets. They had their stated hours for calling at the hotels. St. Henry Street faced our house, and Grant's Hotel was near by. I used to watch the passengers as they arrived and departed. How the number of parcels, travelling bags and trunks were to be disposed of, was a mystery, but the driver, usually good humoured, had a dexterous way of placing them. When all was ready, he cracked his long whip, and the horses went off with speed.

I had the experience of travelling to the Caledonia Springs in one of these conveyances, and enjoyed the journey very much. The coach was comfortable on good springs. There were three seats each holding three persons. There was an interest and sympathy among the passengers which one does not meet with in our days of quick travel. . . .

I remember St. Helen's Island when it was only occupied by the military. I was invited by a lady, the wife of a gentleman in the Commissariat, for a ten days' visit. I was taken over to the island in a garrison boat rowed by soldiers. There were lovely walks, one especially, overarched with the branches of trees grown on either side. The most interesting part, was the military portion with its barracks, armory, magazines and military cemetery. . . .

I remember hearing the gun regularly fired at noon, and at six o'clock. . . .

My visit there recalls pleasant remembrances. When I returned home from this visit my father and mother were much interested in what I had to tell them, for it was quite a privilege to have visited such an exclusive place.

4

A City of Picturesque Contrasts

Not all the marketing in nineteenth-century Montreal was done in the usual market-places, such as the Bonsecours which dominated the last half of the century. Year by year, in the period about 1840, the big double sleighs arrived at Christmas-time from Glengarry, laden with produce. Many Montrealers looked forward to their coming, for they arrived at that time of the year when the island had been cut off from the main-land, waiting for the freezing of the ice-roads. The Glengarry sleighs came over the ice at the west end of the island, where the water froze before it did on the wider stretch to the South Shore. Coming as they did just before Christmas, they seemed to bring an outpouring of the season's plenty. Dealers as well as housewives would be early at the taverns, making their selection from the produce in the sleighs.

John Fraser described the coming of the Glengarry sleighs as he had known them. He remembered seeing squads of twenty-five and sometimes fifty entering St. Joseph Street (now Notre Dame Street West) in the winter's twilight.

John Fraser, born on a farm on the Lower Lachine Road, had much of the lore of the region in his memory. This account of the Glengarry sleighs is to be found on pages 123, 126-35 of his book *Canadian Pen and Ink Sketches* (Montreal, 1890).

The old people of Montreal may have some faint recollection of a Glengarry double sleigh of half a century ago, but to the young of this generation, and even to young Glengarrians of the present day, it will be quite a novelty to them to learn how their worthy grandfathers used to come to town. Therefore, we shall bring them back to those good, quiet old times before the introduction of railways into this Canada of ours. There were two noted annual arrivals in those early days, which caused more talk and created greater excitment on the streets of old Montreal than the arrival now-a-days of an ocean steamer. One was the arrival of the first Indian canoe from the North-West, carrying the news and the letters of a past year from those then nearly Polar regions. The other was the first batch of Glengarry double sleighs to reach "John Grant's," or some other of the Scotch inns or taverns of Montreal, about Christmas week, loaded with all good things to replenish the cellars of the citizens, and to place before the traders in pork, butter, cheese, etc., an opportunity for profitable investment. . . .

We invite the reader to come with us, in retrospect, to a farm house in Lochiel, in the then backwoods of Glengarry. There is a large home-made sleigh standing empty under the barn shed. It is some ten to twelve feet long, four to five feet wide, with sides three to four feet high. The runners were cut from a large birch or elm tree. The whole is "home-made," except the iron on the runners and the necessary nails and bolts. The whippletrees and traces may be the same as used for plough or harrow. This is the old Glengarry double sleigh, all home-made, strong and well built, of which we write.

Now, to the loading — let us take a peep at its contents: Some ten or a dozen small tubs or kegs of butter in the bottom, a dozen or two small cheeses, a few bags of timothy seed, then much prized, a few fowl, turkeys, geese, etc., to fill up gaps, then eight to ten well-fed dressed hogs (Glengarry pork was nearly equal to Irish), besides many little odds and ends, such as home-made socks and mits, then much prized in Montreal, and, maybe, a few extra hides and stray furs collected at the farm-house during the year. This is something after the fashion a Glengarry double sleigh was loaded in the old time before leaving for Montreal; the whole, we suppose, to weigh about 2,500 to 3,000 pounds, representing a cash value from $200 to $250.

The time is the second week of December, with good sleighing; the delay in starting is waiting to hear if the ferries are frozen over; all is now ready. Food for man and horse had to be added to the load. This was some dozen bundles of hay and a few bags of oats for the horses, and a small kist or box containing a good-sized boiled ham and a couple of loaves of bread, with a few other small items, such as a select cheese and a little "croudie" for the men on the road, not forgetting a little half-gallon brown jug, containing something to keep out the bitter cold. By the way, this top load of hay towering high, something like a loaded elephant, served as a nice protection for the men from the cold winds, by making a cozy seat in the centre of it. And if the good wife made up her mind to go down to town, she would be nearly as comfortable as at her own fireside.

The reader might suppose the cost for such a trip of eighty miles would be very expensive. It did not cost over a dollar and a half to reach Montreal. Here it is, an actual fact. The end of the first day found them at the Cedars, a halt having been made at mid-day to water and feed the horses. This cost them nothing; they were fed out of the sleigh supplies. The men also had their food with them, but we shall allow them to indulge in a few pots of beer on the road during the day, costing about a quarter of a dollar. Beer was then cheap — three to four coppers a glass. This was the actual outlay in cash the first day until they reached the Cedars.

The horses had to be stabled at the Cedars, costing a quarter of a dollar for a double stall for the night. The men fed their horses from their own supplies, costing nothing. As for the men (there were always two with a double sleigh) a double bed would cost a shilling, but Glengarrians of that day were accustomed to rough it; and invariably made beds for themselves in a corner of the large old-fashioned bar-room, by using their buffalo robes and blankets, thereby saving a little. We shall, however, suppose they spent a quarter each for beer, or something else, to wash down the food from their supply box.

The first halt the second day was at the Cascades, to water the horses, and sixpence for beer. The next was at St. Annes, to water, and another sixpence for beer. The third was at Pointe Claire, for an hour, to feed horses and men, and we shall allow them a shilling for beer. Lachine is the next halt, to water, and sixpence for beer.

The charges for beer on the road may not have been actually indulged in by the men, but they had to pay about sixpence at each halting-place to the country innkeeper for the use of his shed to water and feed the horses, and for this payment were each entitled to a glass of beer—take it or not.

About sunset, the second day, a long string of double sleighs (Glengarrians always came in squads of twelve or fifteen) might be seen between Dow's brewery and the Tanneries, jogging along at a slow pace of about five miles an hour. If their approach was slow, they made noise enough announcing the coming of the Cameron and the Macdonald men to town.

The reader of to-day never heard the merry cling-clong of the loud-sounding, large Glengarry bells of those days. They could be heard fully half a mile distant. Those Glengarry bells were as characteristic of the people as were their own bagpipes. Highlanders always make a noise by making themselves heard and felt when they come to the front, be it at market town, in the legislative halls, or on the battle-field.

Just as the shades of evening are closing over the unlighted streets of old Montreal, the sleighs are passing down St. Joseph street, some wending their way to John Grant's, on St. Henry street, others to Sandy Shaw's, at the corner of Wellington and Grey Nun street, a few to Widow McBarton's on St. Paul street, opposite to the centre of the present St. Ann's market, and a portion of them finding their way to Jemmy Cameron's, the Glasgow tavern, on the Main street.

There were then a goodly number of Scotch taverns in Montreal, having large stabling. These were the resort of the Glengarrians; they could stable their horses for a quarter of a dollar a day, while they fed them out of their sleigh supplies; therefore costing them a mere trifle for the two or three days they spent in town. The men could live like princes, as they thought, at a cost of half a dollar a day each. This was the charge per day at any of those Scotch taverns.

The morning talk the next day at every breakfast table, rich or poor, was of the arrival of the Glengarry sleighs. People now-a-days, when we have railway trains arriving every hour, can hardly conceive the importance such an arrival was to the old inhabitants of Montreal. Perhaps for a full month previous, the whole outside country had been cut off, waiting the freezing of the rivers and ferries, many articles of country produce becoming scarce and dear . . .

An early visit to the Scotch taverns by the thrifty house-wives of old Montreal, was the first duty of the day. There they found Donald, Evan and Sandy prepared, with all the native dignity of Highlanders, to greet their town customers, and to allow the ladies to inspect their good things, and tubs of butter, cheese, turkeys, etc., soon found ready sale.

Glengarry butter had a special character of being good in those early days, and the first arrivals found ready sale to private families; the traders and merchants picked up the balance. Some of the older Glengarrians who had visited town several times before had learned that sides of pork cut into nice "roasting pieces" found a ready sale; therefore, they had prepared themselves for this demand, by which they profited largely.

Our Glengarry friends soon found their sleighs empty, and their pockets full of good hard silver. We shall allow them to prepare for their return home, after purchasing such needed articles as they required for their houses and their farms, these being mostly in the hardware line, such as axes, saws, nails, etc., but one very common article,

"Liverpool salt," took up most of the sleigh; nearly every sleigh carried half a ton of salt home. This article was cheap, about a shilling a bushel, but one of the most expensive for a farmer to buy from the country merchant, owing to the heavy charge of transport in those early days.

The old Glengarry double sleigh, like the once far-famed mail coach of Old England, is now an institution of the past — a relic of departed days. We shall never again see one on the road. We might use the vulgar phrase, "Their usefulness is gone." Never again shall their loud-sounding bells, once so familiar here, be heard on the streets of Montreal, announcing their welcome arrival during the Christmas week. Those days are gone, never again to return!

Relic of departed days, farewell! The writer has endeavoured to picture one of those sleighs, and its usefulness, to the best of his humble ability. Although not a Glengarrian, he was as familiar in his young days with a Glengarry double sleigh as most Glengarrians. He has seen squads of twenty-five, and sometimes fifty, on the road at one time.

In Montreal in the nineteenth century, while the English-speaking population made its presence evident by the scope and increasing variety of its business enterprises, the French had a presence quite as imposing from the number and size of their religious institutions. These gained all the more status in the city from their antiquity — from the very fact that many were already, even in the nineteenth century, some two hundred years old.

Visitors to Montreal, even when disposed to be sceptical and questioning, would be impressed by the work being carried out by the nuns in the instruction of children, and in their great institutions for the care of the sick, the aged, and orphans. They would be impressed not only by the size of these institutions but also by the fact that the hospitals were open to anyone in need.

One of the best descriptions of these great French-Canadian institutions of charity was written by the English traveller, James Silk Buckingham (1786-1855), who spent an active life in journalism, lecturing and travel. In 1818 he established the *Calcutta Journal*, which was suppressed five years later for its outspoken views. He then founded other journals, including the *Athenæum*, which he sold to Carlyle's friend, John Sterling. From 1832 to 1837 he was the Member of Parliament for the new borough of Sheffield, and advocated such reforms as temperance and the abolition of flogging in the Army and Navy. After 1837 much of his life was spent in travel, and in writing and lecturing on the places he had visited. He has been described as "a man of great kindness of heart and liberality of opinion."

In 1842 Buckingham made a point of visiting Montreal's charitable institutions in turn and inspecting them carefully. His report reveals his satisfaction with what he saw, though he examined the work being done from a Protestant's point of view.

These institutions were still in the old area near the waterfront they had occupied since the French régime. The Hôtel Dieu was on the north side of St. Paul Street, at what is now the corner of St. Sulpice. The Congregation of Notre Dame (the Black Nuns) was on the south side of Notre Dame Street, at the corner of St. Jean Baptiste. The Grey Nunnery was on the south side of Commissioners Street, facing St. Ann's Market (now Place d'Youville).

This account of the visits of this English Protestant traveller to the French-Canadian nunneries of Montreal is taken from his book *Canada, Nova Scotia, New Brunswick and the other British Provinces of North America* . . . (London, 1843), pages 114-17, 119-21.

The most ancient is the Nunnery of the Hotel Dieu, which was founded in 1644, by Madame de Bouillon, for the reception and care of the sick and diseased poor, of all nations, and of both sexes. It is situated nearly in the

centre of the city, and covers a large area of 468 feet by
324. The funds by which it is sustained are derived from
rents of lands and houses, belonging to the Hotel from the
original endowments, assisted occasionally by grants from
the Provincial Legislature. Nothing could exceed the
cleanliness, neatness, and comfort of the several wards
in which the sick and aged are accommodated here; and
the Dispensary of Medicines was the most perfect in its
arrangement that I ever remember to have seen. The
Sisters, as they are called, by whom the establishment is
conducted, are in number thirty-seven, one of whom is the
Superior. They are what are called Cloistered Nuns, never
leaving the building and the garden attached to it, but
devoting themselves entirely to religious worship, and the
care of the sick and infirm. They dress in a black habit,
with a broad collar, plain, but of snowy whiteness, extending over the bosom and neck, a white frontlet covering the brow close down to the eye-brows, and a black
gauze veil thrown back over the head. The ages of those we
saw, varied between thirty and fifty. Their duties are
severe, and their diet scanty and simple. In the chapel
attached to the convent, which is richly ornamented, they
have mass celebrated every day, and offices of devotion at
three separate periods besides. From each of the sick wards
there are large windows leading into galleries of the
chapel, from whence the altar can be seen, and the music
and prayers heard, by those who are too sick or too infirm
to go to the chapel itself. The admissions to the Hospital
are limited only by the extent of their accommodations,
which will receive about a hundred persons. Those who
enter it are supported gratuitously, and supplied with food
and medicine for as long as they may require it; and as

soon as those who are cured leave the Hospital, there are always others to fill their places.

The candidates for the Sisterhood are chiefly Canadians; but sometimes French and Irish. They must be well recommended for piety and morals, and undergo a a probation of five years, after which, if their conduct is approved, they are received into the Sisterhood, and take the black veil, making, at the same time, three vows, one of chastity, one of poverty, and one of seclusion and devotion to the care of the sick and infirm. Two of the Sisters are at all times together, in each ward, day and night, relieving each other in watches of four hours; and none are exempt from this duty except the Lady Superior, whose constant superintendence during the day furnishes her with abundant occupation. They appear to be very happy, and are under no physical restraint, as the gate of the Nunnery is always open in the daytime, and there is nothing to prevent the escape of any Sister who desired it, but no such attempt has ever been made.

The Black Nunnery, or Convent of Notre Dame, is the next in order of date, having been founded in 1653, by Madame Marguerite Burgeois, accompanied by some young ladies whom she brought with her from France, to form a seminary for female education. This Nunnery is also in the centre of the City, fronting the street of Notre Dame, and covering an area of 433 feet by 234. These are not cloistered nuns; though living in community, and making vows of chastity and poverty, they are not secluded, but go out as occasion requires, and attend worship publicly at the cathedral. There is a Superior and eighty Sisters in the whole; but not more than forty are usually resident at the Nunnery; the remainder being sent to the surrounding villages as missionaries, to superintend the education of female children there, and usually going in pairs. At the time of our visit (September 2nd), the pupils had just begun to return to school from the summer vacation; and about half the number only, or eighty, were present. These varied between ten and eighteen years of age; and though chiefly Canadians, included some from New York and other parts of the United States. They were in general good-looking, healthy, clean, dressed in a neat uniform of blue striped gingham, with black silk aprons, and appeared cheerful and happy. Their course of education embraces all the usual branches of useful and ornamental instruction; and from the specimens of music, writing, embroidery, and other productions, that we witnessed, we were disposed to infer that they were well instructed. There are about one hundred and sixty boarders, and forty day-scholars; and the expense of board and tuition does not exceed 20l. sterling per annum. The receipts from education are not quite sufficient to sustain the establishment, as in the villages, the Sisters teach the children of the poor gratuitously; but the deficiency is made up from the funds of the St. Sulpicians; as this Convent has no endowments besides the building and its accessaries. The Sisters dress in a black habit, with a white handkerchief surrounding the face, an apron with dark blue and white stripes, and a black hood and veil. In this dress they are often seen in the streets, and at the cathedral, and hence the name of the Black Nuns is given to them by the inhabitants, from the black habit and veil of the order.

The Grey Nunnery is a larger establishment than either of the preceding, though more recent in point of date. It lies farther removed from the centre of the town, towards the south, and occupies a most agreeable situation, near the banks of the river. . . .

We were received by the nuns with great courtesy and kindness. The Lady Superior, who is Treasurer and Manager of the Estates of the Institution, as well as Directress of all the internal economy of the establishment, was at her desk in the library, making up her accounts, when we arrived; and after a short conversation on the object of our visit, she introduced us to the Sisters, about a dozen of whom were occupying a spacious and agreeable apartment looking out on the St. Lawrence, with a large garden before it, and a pleasant balcony for a promenade, communicating with the room. These were all engaged in needlework of various kinds; but all entered cheerfully into conversation; and we thought we had seldom seen a more ruddy or healthy set of middle-aged ladies between forty and sixty than these. All the emblems of their faith were thickly placed around the room; crucifixes, pictures of saints, representations of miracles and Scriptural scenes; but there was nothing gloomy in their appearance or deportment; on the contrary, they were not merely serene, but cheerful.

We were shown over every part of this establishment, with as little reserve as in either of the others, a privilege which we owed no doubt to the authority of the Superior of the St. Sulpicians, under whose auspices our visit was made, as well as to the influence of the reverend Brother who accompanied us. Here the wards for the sick, the insane, the aged, and the infirm, were all more spacious, more airy, and better fitted with every requisite, than either of those we had visited before; and the neatness and cleanliness of everything we saw excited our admiration. The number of the Sisters is about sixty; their ages vary between thirty and seventy years; their dress is a grey habit, with a neat white cap, white apron, and silver crucifix. They are subject to the same probation or noviciate as the Black Nuns, and make vows of chastity, poverty, and devotion to their duties, when they are adopted into the order; but no vows of solitude or separation from the world. They observe nearly the same discipline as the Sisters of the Hotel Dieu, watching in turns with the sick, the aged, and the insane; of whom they have about a hundred and fifty under their care at present; and training, exercising, and instructing the foundlings and orphans, of whom they have nearly two hundred, from two to twelve years of age. After this period, they find occupation both for the boys and girls, and generally sustain or assist them till they are able to get their own living. They have a pretty island, called the Nun's Island, in the St. Lawrence, a little above the town, which they have had cultivated with grain, vegetables, and fruits; and this, with other lands and houses, yields them a handsome revenue, which they judiciously and benevolently expend in works of the most disinterested charity, to which indeed they devote all their labour and care. The Sisters here, as well as in the other Nunneries, occupy very small bedrooms, with the simplest furniture, and their diet and apparel is all of the plainest kind. They are not stimulated by the admiration of the world, nor rewarded by the praises of mankind; but appear to be solely actuated by sincerely devotional, or religious and benevolent feelings, to the performance of their duties, for which their only reward is an approving conscience.

While Charles Dickens was in Montreal in May, 1842, what impressed him most was the sight of the immigrants on Montreal's quays or coming up on the boat from Quebec. Rasco's hotel, where Dickens was staying, was near the quays, being on St. Paul Street; the old building still stands, now facing the Bonsecours Market. It was a very short distance from Rasco's to the waterfront, for his morning strolls.

Dickens' picture of the immigrants is very different from that given earlier in the century by the anonymous writer in *The Canadian Magazine*. That writer of the eighteen-twenties had viewed them with cynical realism, in all their dirt, noise and disarray. But to Charles Dickens, more emotional and with the new Victorian outlook, the human appeal of this struggle against anxiety and hardship was overwhelming. He saw in these immigrants something close to the main theme of his novels: the plain, cheerful, long-suffering of ordinary people, with all the disadvantages of this world and most of its virtues.

In the spring of the year, vast numbers of emigrants who have newly arrived from England or from Ireland, pass between Quebec and Montreal on their way to the backwoods and new settlements of Canada. If it be an entertaining lounge (as I very often found it) to take a morning stroll upon the quay at Montreal, and see them grouped in hundreds on the public wharfs about their chests and boxes, it is matter of deep interest to be their fellow-passenger on one of these steamboats, and mingling with the concourse, see and hear them unobserved.

The vessel in which we returned from Quebec to Montreal was crowded with them, and at night they spread their beds between decks (those who had beds, at least), and slept so close and thick about our cabin door, that the passage to and fro was quite blocked up. They were nearly all English; from Gloucestershire the greater part; and had had a long winter-passage out; but it was wonderful to see how clean the children had been kept, and how untiring in their love and self-denial all the poor parents were.

Cant as we may, and as we shall to the end of all things, it is very much harder for the poor to be virtuous than it is for the rich; and the good that is in them, shines the brighter for it. In many a noble mansion lives a man, the best of husbands and of fathers, whose private worth in both capacities is justly lauded to the skies. But bring him here, upon this crowded deck. Strip from his fair young wife her silken dress and jewels, unbind her braided hair, stamp early wrinkles on her brow, pinch her pale cheek with care and much privation, array her faded form in coarsely patched attire, let there be nothing but his love to set her forth or deck her out, and you shall put it to the proof indeed. So change his station in the world, that he shall see in those young things who climb about his knee: not records of his wealth and name: but little wrestlers with him for his daily bread; so many poachers on his scanty meal; so many units to divide his every sum of comfort, and farther to reduce its small amount. In lieu of the endearments of childhood in its sweetest aspect, heap upon him all its pains and wants, its sicknesses and ills, its fretfulness, caprice, and querulous endurance: let its prattle be, not of engaging infant fancies, but of cold, and thirst, and hunger: and if his fatherly affection outlive all this, and he be patient, watchful, tender; careful of his children's lives, and mindful always of their joys and sorrows; then send him back to Parliament, and Pulpit, and to Quarter Sessions, and when he hears fine talk of the depravity of those who live from hand to mouth, and labour hard to do it, let him speak up, as one who knows, and tell those holders forth that they, by parallel with such a class, should be High Angels in their daily lives, and lay but humble siege to Heaven at last.

Which of us shall say what he would be, if such realities, with small relief or change all through his days, were his! Looking around upon these people: far from home, houseless, indigent, wandering, weary with travel and hard living: seeing how patiently they nursed and tended their young children: how they consulted ever their wants first, then half supplied their own; what gentle ministers of hope and faith the women were; how the men profited by their example; and how very, very seldom even a moment's petulance or harsh complaint broke out among them: I felt a stronger love and honour of my kind come glowing on my heart, and wished to God there had been many Atheists in the better part of human nature there, to read this simple lesson in the book of Life.

How deep, in the nineteenth century, was the feeling of French Canadians for the life of the countryside and the tradition of the family farm may be sensed in the article in *La Revue Canadienne* where the writer deplored the encroachment of the city on the farms near Mount Royal. He was not simply regretting the changing view. What he saw passing was a way of life that was sound and good, to be replaced by the tawdriness of city ways. What he was writing in 1845 may be compared with what Father Trudeau said in addressing the St. Jean Baptiste Society in Notre Dame Church in 1870, when he warned his listeners that they would lose everything if they once gave up their farms, and lost the tradition of the *habitant*.

Until the middle of the century Montreal had grown east and west along the waterfront, rather than toward the Mountain. The slopes facing the city remained largely covered with orchards. This description of them has been translated from the column headed "Histoire de la Semaine," in *La Revue Canadienne,* October 18, 1845.

Montreal of all cities is known far and wide for the fruit produced in its neighbourhood. In the old days the side of the mountain that looks toward the east was, in particular, covered with magnificent orchards, whose fruit, especially the apples, was superior to anything other countries could offer. The variety of apples was infinite, and one had to be born on the slopes of the mountain to be acquainted with them all. The *fameuse,* the *grise,* the *rainette,* the *bourassa,* the *roseau,* the *calville,* were fruits which could not be found anywhere as perfect as here. But our fine orchards, where we played as children, are becoming fewer and fewer every day, and the quantity of our fruits grows less every year. The quality, moreover, is no longer the same. You scarcely recognize our apples; they are degenerating through the mixing of species.

The expansion of our city is mostly toward the western side of the mountain. The fine country properties have not been spared by the recent building craze. An orchard, to the eyes of the owner, is good for nothing but *building lots.* Look around at the areas near the mountain and you see everywhere signs with "Building Lots" in big letters. The most respectable and oldest families have given up, and are giving up, every year, the patrimony of their fathers — the land still full of reminders of their forbears, the joys and pleasures of the family — to the encroachments of progress. It is a fine thing to preserve an orchard, of some twelve *arpents,* nestled at the foot of the mountain, and commanding a splended view of the city, the river and the countryside as far as the eye can reach, where your father, your grandfather, first saw the light of day, as you did yourself — where they lived happy, peaceful and contented lives, where they died. Here the paths through the grass still bear the imprint of their steps; here are the great trees that shaded their old age; here is the simple and quaint house, the humble home whose every corner holds a memory of the days that are gone. The memory of your mother, of your sisters, dear companions of early years, whom we so often lose as life goes on; all the intimate things of the heart, these possessions, which, we believe, are greater than all other possessions, they are giving up for a little cash.

Moreover, with progress, luxury begins to intrude in the family life. The quiet, retired existence of the parents does not suit the children. They must have display and pretension. They would not be content any longer with the old family house. The children go their own ways, and the family property goes too. It is good for nothing but *building lots*.

Can there be anyone born in Montreal or near Montreal who has not taken part many a time in his life in those wonderful picnics given in the apple-picking season? The air is brisk and bracing, and you have to dress warmly to stay outdoors most of the day. The good mammas and the young girls wrap themselves up in warmly lined overcoats, or ample and comfortable shawls. These simple and care-free costumes, countrified and unadorned, make you admire a woman's charm and style a hundred times more. It is like a diamond — a really fine diamond — which sparkles as much by itself as when surrounded by tinsel.

You arrive at the orchard. You make your way to some big tree, famous among all the others round about for the quantity of fruit it bears each year. . . . Gnarled like the ancient it is, its branches stretch out, weighed down by abundance and supported with poles. With the measures and baskets strewing the grass, the ladders are put up. The fruit awaits you. Get to work! For, you remember, to have any real pleasure, one needs to work. It is necessary, my little girl, to go quite a way up into the tree to have the fun of letting a big apple drop on a boy friend's head, and then to seem very busy, as if it was pure accident, and to laugh up your sleeve. Work hard to fill your measure before the others, then pretend to be very tired, lie down on the grass at the foot of a tree and laugh at the slow-pokes.

The open air and the exercise give you the glow of health. The most lively well-being, the silliest merriment, the heartiest enjoyment always go with apple-picking. The work goes on amid crazy sayings, double-meanings and practical jokes (the pun was unknown in those happy days).

You took the greatest care in gathering the fruit. I even recall some orchards where apples were picked with gloves, so punctures from finger-nails would not spoil them. There was the first choice, the apple *par excellence*, its skin clear and without blemish, soft and silken. There was the second choice, and the third. Before being placed in the measure, the fruit was closely inspected. By taking this kind of care, the quality of the fruit was assured, and it would keep a long time.

When the church bells rang out the noon-hour, we would say the Angelus, and sit down to dinner (dinner at five or six p.m. was then unknown). A table of grass, simple dishes, plenty of good appetite, a little wine, and smiling faces — that was the kind of dinner we had. Afterwards we would chat, sing, dance on the grass; then we would go back to work. When the sun was setting, and the air was becoming sharper and even cold, we made ready to return home. As we came down we would look at the lovely effect in the sky as the golden shafts fell on the gathering clouds and the purple-red of the twilight, or on the gleaming steeples and fiery roofs of the city.

Then we came home. In the house the fun went on. When supper was over, the blaze on the hearth warmed the heart and the chilled hands and feet. We ended the day and the evening with a big country-dance, and everyone had the privilege of dancing any way he liked and as long as he liked.

Such were the simple pleasures and recreations of autumn in the old days. Today they do not pick apples at "family gatherings;" their amusements are very different from that. They are affected, stuck up, dressed in the latest styles, like fashion plates, and strut about the streets. They find their satisfaction in their grand airs, in ways so extravagant as to be absurd, in an attitude that is pretension itself. They have banished the open-hearted gaiety, the easy-goingness of other days, under the pretext of improving our manners. Let us admit it, is it not so?

Montreal was a uniquely attractive North American city in the eyes of many visitors in the mid-century. It interested them with its contrasts. Here was a city surging with growth — a railroad centre, with fine wharves and confident new buildings, a city full of forward-looking bustle. Yet here also was a city venerable like one of the Old World, the authority of the Church evident, with the spires and the ringing of bells, the long nunnery walls, and the vast Notre Dame Church — always "the Cathedral" to visitors — with its subdued religious light, candles in holy places, and voices chanting at sunset.

How attractive such a city could seem appears in the picture of it by Lieutenant-Colonel B. W. A. Sleigh. He had been born in Montreal but had been away so long amidst other scenes that when he returned as an officer of the 77th Regiment all seemed striking and novel to his eyes. He writes here in the lively, rich-toned, picturesque style that Montreal often evoked in its visitors.

These passages, which appear to have been written about 1846, with additions of a few years' later date, form pages 233-35, 237-41 of his book *Pine Forests or Hacmatack Clearings; or Travel, Life and Adventure in the British North American Provinces* (London, 1853).

At five we were on board the Montreal steamer. The bell tolled, and, punctual to her time, away she flew, high pressure, up the river, towards that city. There were a great many lady passengers on board, and our band, which was a most excellent one, charmed them with a variety of selected opera pieces; while dancing passed away the evening most delightfully. The passage-money from Quebec to Montreal was then only one dollar, which included a most excellent supper, and a very comfortable berth.

It was terribly hot during the night, and at four A.M. I was glad to leave my cabin for the promenade deck, to enjoy the cool and fragrant breeze of early morning. The scenery between Quebec and Montreal assumes a remarkable aspect: bold mountain-ranges give place to luxuriantly cultivated lowlands, teeming with life and the rich resources of agricultural industry. The whole country is studded, as far as the eye can see, with substantial houses, white as snow, surrounded by orchards and judiciously-arranged plantations, and here and there a glittering church-steeple emerging from the groves of greenwood by which those sacred edifices are almost invariably belted.

The waving corn-fields, and rustle of the wheaten sheafs, add tenfold to the beauties of Nature's works, which envelope this charming vista of rural abundance. Village after village studs the margins of the river on either side, which sometimes widens, and then resumes its natural breadth....

At seven o'clock we approached Montreal, which stood out boldly in the distance, presenting one mass of glittering steeples, domes, and massive stone wharves, fully a mile in extent, and the most costly and substantial in North America. Shipping of every size and nation, crowds of steamers, American and English, bateaus, canoes, timber-rafts, schooners in full sail, all covered the surface of the river; and the city, with its dark stone buildings and iron shutters, gave an impression of ancient grandeur; while towards the west rose the Mountain, above six hundred feet high, along whose base, and upward, were charming houses and villa residences of the gentry.

Montreal is six hundred miles from Cape Gaspe, and one hundred and eighty from Quebec. Its position is one of vast commercial importance, standing, as it does, in the centre of all the carrying trade of the Canadas with the Lower Provinces and United States. At the present time, this city, through the numerous lines of railroad radiating from it, is placed in close connection with the Atlantic ports. There are now lines running to Boston, New York, and Portland: thus she is connected with three ports, each with lines of steamers to Europe. Montreal is further united by rail with Toronto and Quebec. You can go through to Boston or New York in eighteen hours; it could be done in twelve by express. It will thus be seen that this city is in a position to become one of the first in North America. As it is, the regularity and magnificence of its buildings, its wharves, public edifices, and business carried on, have placed it in a position of the very first commercial importance. . . .

Having got through my day's work, I rejoined my wife at Doneganie's [Donegana's] Hotel, a magnificent establishment in Notre Dame Street, but which was afterwards burnt down. . . . Everything was conducted in this hotel in the first style: the furniture was superb, and the attendance, all French waiters, most admirable, while the *cuisine* was of the most *recherché* character.

In walking over the city, I could not but remark the beauty of some of the shops and the extent of the streets: Great St. James's-street would reflect credit on London, and the marble edifices of some of the banks were really most imposing. The Roman Catholic Cathedral is the largest in America, and the turrets can be seen towering over the city. Its interior decorations are very costly, and the high altar, after St. Peter's at Rome, is as fine a thing as could be seen in Europe. The church is 255 feet long and 134 broad, and the walls attain an altitude of 112 feet. There are seven chapels and altars, and nine grand aisles. The pulpit is a fac-simile of Strasburg Cathedral. The east window, of stained glass, over the high altar, is 70 feet high and 33 feet broad, while all the other windows are 36 feet high by 10 broad. An idea can therefore be entertained of the superb appearance the interior presents. The church will contain 12,000 persons.

When I first entered the Cathedral, the solemn tone of the organ at Vespers, the choristers' chants, the candles burning on the numerous altars, refulgent with gold and costly gems, the sombre and subdued light, reflected in a thousand prismatic colours from the stained windows, and mellowed by the rays of the setting sun, while the gentle tones of female voices, the Nuns of the Hôtel Dieu and Sœurs Gris (Grey Sisters) pouring forth from their hidden shrines strains of sweet melody, in concert with the fine voices of the monks, filled me with a religious awe, and impressed me with the grandeur of the scene.

The religious establishments in Montreal exceed in extent, if possible, those of Quebec. The Hôtel Dieu, the St. Sulpician Seminary, the nunnery of Notre Dame, and the nunnery of the Grey Sisters, are the principal, all with hospitals attached, and they are kept in the most perfect state of cleanliness and order, while the uniformly kind and tender solicitude of those amiable ladies, who have given up all, to tend the sick, 'the widow, the fatherless and distressed,' cannot be too highly commended. To obtain admission as a patient to the hospitals attached to the nunneries, it is only necessary to show the presence of God's hand, in striking down with sickness and disease the humble supplicant for the balm which shall heal. No inquiry as to faith or creed is made, and the Protestant is received, and as tenderly nursed as the Catholic communicant. The sick have not to go on crutches to governors of hospitals or purse-proud millionnaires, to ask for tickets of recommendation, and then, morning after morning, in cold, fog, and rain, herd together in a damp passage, awaiting the death or cure of an inmate for the chance of admission.

Handsome equipages, with liveried servants, dash along the streets, while well-dressed ladies, *à la Parisienne*, give an air to the favourite promenades of a fashionable and opulent people. . . .

I went to see the regiments in garrison mount guard and troop the colours, in the Champ de Mars, an extensive parade-ground in the heart of the city, surrounded by rows of old poplars. The number of well-dressed people and the assemblage of beauty would reflect credit on an English city. Indeed, in Montreal, you cannot fancy you are in America; everything about it conveys the idea of a substantial, handsomely-built European town, with modern improvements of half English, half French architecture, and a mixed population of the two races. The *habitants'* strange dress, with their grey cloth *capots,* with the scarlet sash tied round the waist, and *bonnet bleu,* with Indian mocassins, tastefully worked in beads of various colours, is certainly foreign. The Canadian women look very pretty, with the *mantelet* of grey-coloured cloth, stuff petticoat, and head-dress — mob or Normandy caps; and their feet, which are very small, look so saucy in those elegant little mocassins!

There are also to be seen stalking about numbers of Indians, with their squaws, their children tied to their backs in wooden cases, almost invariably sucking a piece of pork fat, tied with a string to avert the chance of suffocation. Canadian voyagers formed another motley group, with their half Indian dresses, bronzed faces, and flaringly-striped cotton shirts. Hunters, from the Hudson's Bay Company's regions, come in with peltries, to return with provisions for some distant fort. Then there is your regular Yankee "b'hoy," belonging to the river steamers, or on tours of trade with the natives. Throw into this crowd an odd monk, in his sombre vestments, a lady of charity, hidden by a veil from vulgar gaze, swiftly proceeding, with head bended, on a tour of mercy or kindly mission, and Highland soldiers in the kilt, Infantry soldiers with the (*becoming?*) Prince Albert Chacos, Artillerymen, Sappers and Miners, Rifles, Officers, Aides-de-camp, gold-lace, cocked-hats and feathers, and you have a fair description of the motley masses, who every day swarm the streets of Montreal.

The simplicity of medical education in the eighteen-forties is seen in Dr. Duncan C. MacCallum's account of his days as a student at McGill. Yet the McGill medical faculty, in its association with the Montreal General Hospital, had a high reputation even from its early years. The fact is that medical knowledge was itself limited at the time, and good teachers, even with simple methods and means, could provide sound instruction.

The quaintness of Dr. MacCallum's account is heightened by the fact that he was studying medicine at McGill during the years after the McGill governors had persuaded the medical professors to move their classes from quarters in town near the hospital to the building (corresponding to the centre of the present Arts Building) which had just been erected on the campus. The medical professors were aware that the campus was so far "from the centre of population" that its use would "be attended with very serious inconvenience, if not insuperable difficulty." But in 1845 the move took place, largely because the medical faculty was being offered space in the new building free of charge.

Dr. MacCallum describes his struggles to reach the building on snowy mornings and its weird loneliness at night, "far removed from other dwellings." The medical faculty moved back toward the centre of the city in 1851, to a building on Côté Street.

Duncan MacCallum, after graduating from McGill in 1850, studied in London, Edinburgh and Dublin. From 1854 till his retirement in 1877 he held a series of McGill appointments, in such different fields as clinical surgery, clinical medicine, midwifery, and the diseases of women and children; and this in itself is another illustration of the versatility that was still possible in that era.

His account of his experiences as a medical student appeared in the article, "Reminiscences of the Medical School of McGill University," in *The McGill University Magazine*, April, 1903.

88

In the year 1847 when I entered McGill College as a student of medicine, there were two buildings on the University grounds, one of which, surmounted by a cupola and forming at present the central part of the Arts' building, was occupied by the two Faculties existing at the time — the Faculties of Arts and Medicine. The second, now the east wing of the Arts' building, was the residence of several university officials. These buildings were reached from Sherbrooke Street by a road at the side of the grounds, now forming University Street. East of this entrance towards St. Lawrence Street there were a few scattered buildings. On the south side of Sherbrooke Street, extending from the McGill grounds to Dorchester Street and from Union Avenue westward to Mountain Street, there were open fields and gardens in a state of cultivation, and a few dwellings — the two most notable of which were "Burnside Cottage," the former residence of the Hon. James McGill, the Founder of the University, and the "Protestant Infants' Home," on St. Catherine Street.

A small stream of water passed through the grounds. It entered from the east at a point just above the situation of the present University Street entrance, and was increased in volume by the water from a spring which was situated near where the Macdonald Engineering Building now stands. It then passed down the campus and across Sherbrooke Street, where it was joined by another small stream from the south-west. It then took a course towards the city, passing close to "Burnside Cottage." It is probable that the relative position of this stream and the Hon. James McGill's cottage was the origin of the name of "Burnside" given to the latter.

All the lectures, with the exception of the clinical lectures and those on chemistry, were delivered in the central Arts' building. . . .

As the first lecture of the day, that of Dr. MacCulloch on Midwifery, was delivered from eight to nine o'clock a.m., the student had to rise early on the cold winter mornings, often before daylight, in order to dress himself and breakfast to enable him to reach the college in time for the commencement of the lecture. At all times the roads were heavy and not favourable to rapid walking, and not unfrequently heavy snow-storms rendered them almost impassable for many days. This was especially the case with the road leading from Sherbrooke Street to the college. This locality was much exposed to any prevailing wind, which piled the snow in drifts, and made it impossible to reach the college until they had been partially removed by a shovel brigade. On such occasions our kind-hearted Professor, Dr. MacCulloch, who drove to the college in one of those winter sleighs known as a berline or cariole, and which are now used, but of a larger size, by the carters of Montreal, would pick up as many struggling students as he could possibly accommodate, and drive them to the lecture. I have seen as many as half-a-dozen students at one time occupying and clinging to his sleigh.

Another great inconvenience resulting from the distant and isolated position of the college building, was the difficulty the student laboured under of prosecuting his studies in Practical Anatomy during the early part of the night. Dissections and demonstrations were made only at stated times during the morning and afternoon of the day. There evidently existed a marked disinclination on the part of both demonstrator and student to work at night in the highest story of a lonely building, far removed from other dwellings, imperfectly heated, and lighted by candles — the light being barely sufficient to render the surrounding darkness visible.

Having occupied for two seasons the position of Prosector to the Professor of Anatomy, I had to prepare, during the greater part of the session, the dissections of the parts which were to be the subject of the Professor's lecture on the following day. This necessitated my passing several hours, usually from nine to twelve o'clock at night, in the dismal, foul-smelling dissecting room, my only company being several partially dissected subjects, and numerous rats which kept up a lively racket, coursing over and below the floor and within the walls of the room. Their piercing and vicious shrieks as they fought together, the thumping caused by their bodies coming into forcible contact with the floor and walls, and the rattling produced by their rush over loose bones, furnished a variety of sounds that would have been highly creditable to any old-fashioned haunted house. I must acknowledge that the eeriness of my surroundings was such that I sometimes contemplated a retreat, and was prevented from carrying it into effect only by a sense of duty and a keen dislike to being chaffed by my fellow-students for having cowardly deserted my work.

Another existing circumstance, namely, the great distance of the college from the Montreal General Hospital, was a source of annoyance and dissatisfaction to the student, as it seriously interfered with the time allotted for his dinner or mid-day meal. The last lecture in the morning series was delivered between the hours of eleven and twelve. The first of the afternoon series was delivered between two and three o'clock. The student had, therefore, only two hours at his disposal to walk from the college to the hospital, make the visit to the hospital wards, dine, and return to the college in time for the lecture at two o'clock. . . .

It was customary at this time for the student to be indentured to a practising physician, or, if not so bound notarially, to make a private arrangement with him to be allowed to study in his office and to be considered as his pupil. For this privilege a fee of one hundred dollars was usually demanded. Apart from the *éclat* which was supposed to be attached to the position of student under a popular physician, and the belief of the possibility of the patron being able to forward the interests of his pupils, there were, as a rule, few advantages derived from this association. It is true that, in exceptional cases, if the physician had a large *clientèle* and took a warm interest in his students, he could, by arranging their studies, occasionally examining them on the work done, and directing them in the routine of office work, be of material assistance to them. The office work of a physician in large practice, however, offered an excellent opportunity to acquire much practical knowledge. As, with few exceptions, physicians prescribed and dispensed their own medicines, the articled student had the opportunity of making up all the prescriptions. He compounded pills, a variety of which were always kept prepared for use, and he made the different tinctures and ointments. He had the privilege, also, of assisting at minor surgical operations, such as were performed in the office, of making physical examinations, of applying tests; in short, office practice offered the same facilities for acquiring practical knowledge, although in a minor degree, that the out-door practice of an hospital or the practice of a dispensary affords.

The *personnel* of the class was markedly different from what it is in present times. Then, a large proportion of the students were men verging on, or who had passed, middle age. Indeed, several of them were married men and the heads of families. There was sufficient of the youthful, however, to keep things lively. "Footing Suppers," practical jokes, and special country excursions to secure material for practical anatomy, were of frequent occurrence. The last, involving as it did a certain amount of danger, commended itself particularly to the daring spirits of the class, who were always ready to organize and lead an excursion having that object in view. These excursions were not at all times successful, and the participators in them were sometimes thwarted in their attempts, and had to beat a precipitate retreat to save themselves from serious threatened injury. They contributed, moreover, to the unpopularity of the medical student.

"Footing Suppers" were functions of the simplest and most unpretentious character. Each new matriculant was expected, although many failed to conform to the arrangement, to select an evening on which to entertain his fellow students, the entertainment consisting generally in furnishing biscuits and beer — the old time-endorsed "cakes and ale." In partaking of these, smoking, relating humorous stories, chaffing each other and singing rousing songs, the evening usually passed with much *bonhommie.* But sometimes they were rather boisterous, or, at least, noisy and exciting. They certainly could not lay the slightest claim to be classed with "the feast of reason and the flow of soul." Happily, these "Footing Suppers" have been relegated to the realms of forgetfulness, and have been succeeded by the decorous, high-toned, respectable dinners, conversaziones, and balls of the present day.

The examinations for the degree of the University were conducted orally, ten minutes being allowed to each examiner. The janitor, supplied with a watch and a large bell, was placed in the hall outside the door of the library, the room in which the examinations took place. At the expiration of each ten minutes he rang the bell, and the candidates went from one examiner to another. This was repeated until the student had completed the round of examining professors. Immediately on the termination of the examinations, the professors met and decided then and there the fate of the candidates. The latter, in the meantime, waited in the college in a rather painful state of suspense. They were summoned separately before the professors, and the result, favourable or unfavourable, in each case made known to the individual. It did one good to see the effect which the announcement had on the successful student — the straightening of the body, the brightening of the eye, and the happy smile radiating rapidly over his face as he rushed around giving each professor an energetic pump-handle shake of the hand, followed, as he disappeared through the door of the room and was received by the crowd of waiting students, by a shout that made the college ring. On the other hand, I believe the professors never passed a more miserable quarter of an hour than when announcing his failure to the unfortunate candidate. It was painful to a degree to witness the depression produced by the announcement, especially when contrasted with the joy and elation of the successful man. The decision, as a rule, was received quietly, and, without a word, the unfortunate one, with bowed head and with countenance painfully expressive of deep disappointment, slipped from the room and was received silently by the waiting crowd of sympathizing students.

5

Views of Mid-Century Montreal

One of the oddest confrontations of nineteenth-century Montreal came when Henry David Thoreau visited Notre Dame Church in Place d'Armes. No man, it might have seemed, could have found himself in a place less comprehensible or acceptable.

Thoreau was not only a New England Yankee; he was independent and opinionated far beyond even New England's standards. He carried his refusal to conform to the extent of refusing to vote or pay taxes. He refused to go to any church, but sought his wisdom in a hut near Concord, in the woods by Walden Pond — a hut he built for himself at a cost of twenty-eight dollars. For him the still, small voice — the voice of truth and wisdom — was the voice of Nature.

When Thoreau came to Montreal in 1850 it was on his first trip outside the United States. He had come to see and judge for himself, insisting on an uncluttered view. And for simplicity's sake, he carried his baggage in a brown-paper parcel.

What would a philosopher — so naturalistic and austere — think of vast Notre Dame Church, hoarding, as it did, the traditions and symbols of the centuries and exalting the authority of Rome? Thoreau's answer, independent in an unexpected way, is in his book *A Yankee in Canada* (Boston,

1866) , Chapter I (pages 14-17 in the edition published by
Houghton, Mifflin & Co., Boston and New York, 1896) .

It was early in the afternoon when we stepped ashore.
With a single companion, I soon found my way to the
church of Notre Dame. I saw that it was of great size and
signified something. It is said to be the largest ecclesiastical
structure in North America, and can seat ten thousand. It
is two hundred and fifty-five and a half feet long, and the
groined ceiling is eighty feet above your head. The Catholic are the only churches which I have seen worth remem-
bering, which are not almost wholly profane. I do not
speak only of the rich and splendid like this, but of the
humblest of them as well. Coming from the hurrahing
mob and the rattling carriages, we pushed aside the listed
door of this church, and found ourselves instantly in an
atmosphere which might be sacred to thought and religion, if one had any. There sat one or two women who
had stolen a moment from the concerns of the day, as they
were passing; but, if there had been fifty people there, it
would still have been the most solitary place imaginable.
They did not look up at us, nor did one regard another.
We walked softly down the broad-aisle with our hats in
our hands. Presently came in a troop of Canadians, in
their homespun who had come to the city in the boat with
us, and one and all kneeled down in the aisle before the
high altar to their devotions, somewhat awkwardly, as
cattle prepare to lie down, and there we left them. As if
you were to catch some farmer's sons from Marlboro, come
to cattle-show, silently kneeling in Concord meeting-house
some Wednesday! Would there not soon be a mob peeping
in at the windows? It is true, these Roman Catholics,

97

priests and all, impress me as a people who have fallen far behind the significance of their symbols. It is as if an ox had strayed into a church and were trying to bethink himself. Nevertheless, they are capable of reverence, but we Yankees are a people in whom this sentiment has nearly died out, and in this respect we cannot bethink ourselves even as oxen. I did not mind the pictures nor the candles, whether tallow or tin. Those of the former which I looked at appeared tawdry. It matters little to me whether the pictures are by a neophyte of the Algonquin or the Italian tribe. But I was impressed by the quiet religious atmosphere of the place. It was a great cave in the midst of a city; and what were the altars and the tinsel but the sparkling stalactics, into which you entered in a moment, and where the still atmosphere and the sombre light disposed to serious and profitable thought? Such a cave at hand, which you can enter any day, is worth a thousand of our churches which are open only Sundays, — hardly long enough for an airing, — and then filled with a bustling congregation, — a church where the priest is the least part, where you do your own preaching, where the universe preaches to you and can be heard. I am not sure but this Catholic religion would be an admirable one if the priest were quite omitted. I think that I might go to church myself sometimes some Monday, if I lived in a city where there was such a one to go to. In Concord, to be sure, we do not need such. Our forests are such a church, far grander and more sacred. We dare not leave *our* meeting-houses open for fear they would be profaned. Such a cave, such a shrine, in one of our groves, for instance, how long would it be respected? For what purposes would it be entered, by such baboons as we are? I think of its value not only to religion, but to philosophy and to poetry; besides a reading-room, to have a thinking-room in every city! Perchance the time will come when every house even will have not only its sleeping-rooms, and dining-room, and talking-room or parlor, but its thinking-room, also, and the architects will put it into their plans. Let it be furnished and ornamented with whatever conduces to serious and creative thought. I thought I should not object to the holy water, or any other simple symbol, if it were consecrated by the imagination of the worshippers. . . .

As for the Protestant churches, here or elsewhere, they did not interest me, for it is only as caves that churches interest me at all, and in that respect they were inferior.

When Henry Birks was interviewed near his eighty-second birthday in 1922 his recollections, like those of most merchants, were of two kinds: first, he recalled his early days in his line of business; and then he recalled his life as a small boy.

Born in Montreal in 1840, son of John Birks, a chemist, who had come from England eight years earlier, Henry Birks entered the old firm of Savage and Lyman, watchmakers and jewellers. Their store was on Notre Dame Street, where he recalled working by the light of sperm-oil lamps. He was admitted to partnership in 1868, but Savage and Lyman were overwhelmed in the world depression of the eighteen-seventies and went into voluntary liquidation. To Henry Birks the task of liquidation was assigned. He performed it so capably that it led to the formation of a new company, to be carried on in the Savage and Lyman tradition but under the name of Henry Birks.

In his store on St. Catherine Street at Phillips Square, his reminiscences were given in the form of an interview to the Montreal *Gazette*, and were published on November 22, 1922. The only deletions are of the subheadings in the newspaper item, which are indicated by four dots.

99

Sixty-five years of business life in Montreal is the record attained by Henry Birks, founder and president of Henry Birks and Sons, Limited, who on November 30 celebrates his eighty-second birthday. A pleasant coincidence is that at almost the same time falls the sixty-fifth anniversary of Mr. Birks' entrance into business. To commemorate this, special displays have been arranged by the Birks store for Friday and Saturday, November 24 and 25.

In spite of his age, Mr. Birks still takes a lively personal interest in the jewellery business which bears his name. He is in attendance at the Phillips Square store almost every day, meeting friends and acquaintances with the same cheery smile that greeted the patrons of Savage and Lyman in 1857.

Savage and Lyman, founded in 1818 by George Savage, a skilled watchmaker from London, were at that time Montreal's leading jewellers. Their place of business, at 40 Notre Dame street east, was considered the finest retail store on the continent. Today it would be considered a very unpretentious little establishment. Coal oil was unknown, electricity unthought of, and gas but little used. The lighting in the store was supplied by three lamps fed with sperm oil.

In a discussion concerning the goods most favored in those days, Mr. Birks remarked yesterday that costly and exclusive lines were practically unknown in Montreal. It was considered highly extravagant for the fiance of those days to invest as much as $100 in an engagement ring. The usual purchase of this kind involved $25 or $50. Many modern lovers may find cause to regret the costly change in customs and values produced by the passage of sixty-five years. Almost all jewellery was equally modest in price. "There was no manufacturing of jewellery in Canada during my early association with the business," observed Mr. Birks. "It was almost all imported from London, the favorite pieces being bracelets an inch wide, large round or oval brooches about one and a half inches in diameter, and earrings one to two inches long."

"Despite the low prices of jewellery at that time, Montrealers of today have a distinct advantage over the past generation. Indeed, everything we sell, with the exception of precious stones, which have increased in value, is at least half the price it was sixty-five years ago. For example, our fathers and grandfathers had to pay much more for their timekeepers. The cheapest silver watch sold for about $25, while the least expensive gold watch was valued at $75. Clocks were equally costly." . . .

Even in those days there were some very clever and daring attempts at jewellery robberies. In this connection Mr. Birks tells a story from his early experience:

"A very polished and refined man from Paris came to Montreal about the year 1858. He visited the store a number of times and made friends with me. One day he came in about half-past eight and said that his wife was ill in the St. Lawrence Hall, then the fashionable hotel. He wanted to give her a piece of jewellery, and asked me to accompany him to the hotel, taking some of our best pieces so that his wife might make a selection. So I accompanied him to the hall, bringing with me a parcel of jewellery, and was shown into a waiting room adjoining the bedroom.

"My 'friend' took the parcel into the bedroom apparently for his wife to see her gift. I was sharp enough to look through the crack of the door and I saw his shadow on the floor. Seemingly he was talking to someone who was in bed. I was nervous but felt diffident about going into the room. Finally, however, he delayed so long that I became very uneasy, looked in, and saw that there was no one there. The man had slipped downstairs, escaping through a side door with my parcel of jewellery valued at $1,000.

"A thousand dollars may not seem a great sum to the people of today, but to the junior clerk of 1858 it was a great deal of money. So I immediately made plans to recover the stolen goods.

"The only railroad leading to the United States was one going from Caughnawaga to the American border. [This was not the only railway line leading from the shore opposite Montreal to the United States, though it was an important one.] Since there were no telegraph wires, I took a policeman and drove to Lachine. We had hardly reached our destination when we met a carter coming back with an empty carriage. He told us that his fare was the man we were in search of, and that he had crossed to Caughnawaga. We could get no trace of him at first, but after a time I found that he had walked along the track toward the border. We drove on, and, as we crossed the track at St. Isidore, discovered the man walking up the track with the parcel under his arm. We brought him back to town, and he was sentenced to seven years in the penitentiary, where he died." . . .

In 1849, Mr. Birks' father, John Birks, lived on Cathcart street, on the site of the present New Birks Building. At that time west of what is now Phillips Square there were only two buildings, one the home of a Mr. Ross, the other the Protestant Orphan Asylum. Sir Hugh Allan had a fine house where St. James Methodist Church now

Immigrants at the Montreal waterfront with the old Bonsecours Church in the background. A painting by William Raphael.

Engraved from James Duncan's drawing, 1839

The "Fort des Messieurs" of the Sulpicians on the Priests' Farm, showing the towers that still stand on Sherbrooke Street.

Richard Dillon's view of Montreal at the beginning of the nineteenth century, showing the old fortifications wall.

Voyageurs taking a canoe up a rapids — a test of strength and skill. From the drawing by P. J. Bainbrigge, 1838.

stands. Phillips Square, where the Birks store is located, was the bed of a pond. "When I was a boy," said Mr. Birks, "we used to sail there on rafts. Later, in 1855, the site was purchased by the Rev. William Bond, afterward Archbishop Bond, for less than 25¢ a foot. A stream, from which Burnside Place draws its name, came down from the mountain and ran across Sherbrooke street about where University street is today, to the site of our present store. It then made a turn flowing to what was the Roman Catholic burying ground, near the location of the Windsor Hotel. From there it ran southward to the river."

["]Phillips Place was surrounded by a high fence and was a mass of trees, too thick to even see through. A narrow lane ran through it, and, about seventy years ago, a man hanged himself there. The fact that a man had been found hanging from one of the trees in this grove made it a place of much interest to us boys.

["]At that time Dorchester street was open only from Beaver Hall Square to University street and from Mountain street westward. On the western section of the street "Le Grand Chemin du Roi" of French days, the Hon. John Moffatt, one of the notable figures of the time, had a house in Weredale Park. Covering part of the unopened section of Dorchester street there was a pasture in which a man named Cunningham used to keep cows. Being fond of tricks, as most boys are, I often chased these cows. In turn, Mr. Cunningham chased me with a stick.["]

St. James street and St. Antoine street were, at that time, the main residential districts and had very few stores. Most of the shops were located on St. Paul and Notre Dame streets. Another section in which many prominent people had their homes was between Wellington and

Grey Nuns streets in Griffintown. The great hotel of those days was the St. Lawrence Hall, where many famous characters sojourned during visits to Montreal.

"Sports and amusements were much different from those indulged in by the young people of today," Mr. Birks remarked. "We had no moving picture theatres and no cabarets. Our diversions were very simple indeed. In the season I used to shoot foxes on the mountain and in the winter we were fond of sliding from where Pine avenue now lies in the section between Peel and University street."

Before the building of the bridges between Montreal and the South Shore, the ice itself formed the bridge used by Montrealers to reach the mainland. The season of the ice-bridges was brief. The ice did not form from shore to shore — or "take," as it was called — till about the middle of January, and it grew rotten in the spring sun about the end of March. The ice did not freeze smoothly, but in slopes, peaks and humps. A road had to be cut through it for some two miles; and to guide travellers, it was marked out with fir branches.

The opening of Victoria Bridge at the end of 1859 (it was officially opened the next year) did not mean the end of the ice bridges. The Victoria Bridge was the private property of the Grand Trunk Railway; it had accommodation for its trains only, none for other vehicles or for foot-passengers. Not till 1899 was Victoria Bridge remodelled for general traffic.

The ice-bridges were an exciting and dangerous novelty in the eyes of visitors, nor were the dangers entirely imaginary. An English traveller, William H. G. Kingston (1814-1880) , visiting Montreal on his wedding trip in January, 1854, crossed by sleigh over the ice to Montreal at Bout de l'Ile and then was one of the first that year to pass over the newly formed ice-bridge to St. Lambert.

He was a prolific and fluent writer, with a good eye for detail. He had worked for a time in his father's business in Portugal, before turning to writing as a career. He wrote so many novels, boys' stories, travel books, and books on emigration that by the time of his death they filled 9½ pages of the British Museum's catalogue.

He wrote of Montreal's ice-bridges on pages 248-50 and 269-71 of volume two of his book *Western Wanderings or, a Pleasure Tour in the Canadas* (London, 1856).

A stage of sixteen miles took us to Bou de l'Isle, the post-house, close to the river. Leaving it at about half-past ten we shot down a steep bank, and found ourselves crossing a wide arm of the St. Lawrence, or rather the Ottawa, which forms the eastern boundary of the island of Montreal after it has washed its northern shore. This was the first day it had been passable for some time, as a determined thaw had rendered it rotten; but the previous night's frost had again frozen it hard. We hoped sincerely that it was sufficiently strong; but we had our misgivings as we advanced towards the centre of the wide, icy plain — for should we break through, the perfect hopelessness of escape struck us forcibly. However, I do not mean to say that the idea troubled us much, for we were too much interested with the novelty of the scene as we trotted gaily along for upwards of a mile, shielding our noses from the bitter wind till we reached the extreme end of the island of Montreal. Here we saw our driver, who was a stupid fellow, wavering as to where he should land; and looking out ahead, I observed a considerable quantity of water between us and the shore. However, some Canadians with a sleigh before us cried out, "N'ayez pas peur!" and on we dashed and splashed through it, our horses' legs sinking through the ice, and in another instant were on hard ground, not a little to our satisfaction. . . .

The road as we neared Montreal was almost bare of

snow, but very slippery with ice. The river presented a very curious appearance. Its whole surface up and down, as far as we could see, was covered with huge broken masses of ice, two and three feet thick, piled one over the other in confused heaps, as if they had been trying to overleap each other; or like a terror-stricken crowd overtaken as they are endeavouring to escape from the destroyer. A bright sun shining on the sparkling snow, a smooth, civilised road, and numerous gaily-caparisoned sleighs, made Montreal look clean and cheerful, as with no little satisfaction, at about one o'clock, we drove up to Donegana's Hotel; and in a few minutes were comfortably settled in as nice apartments as we could desire, congratulating ourselves on the happy termination of this part of our journey. . . .

JANUARY, *Tuesday* 10th. — We got up at half-past six in readiness for our journey, and found the thermometer 10° below zero, with a strong wind and snow falling thickly, — no very pleasant prospect, considering the two miles we had to journey across the ice, which had taken a few days before over the St. Lawrence, and was now said to be safe. There was, however, some novelty, and no little excitement, in the undertaking, and we had, on commencing our travels, determined not to be hindered from doing anything which might serve us as a topic of conversation in future days. As soon as we had breakfasted, two sleighs came to the door, one to convey us, the other our luggage, across the St. Lawrence to the railway station at St. Lambert's.

Passing through the few streets which divide Donegana's comfortable hotel from the river, we reached the quays, sliding off which, down an inclined plane, we embarked on the rough ocean of ice which covered the river. The scene was wild, obscure, and dismal in the extreme; and as we turned off the street to enter on this apparently pathless expanse of ice, which resembled a raging sea arrested in its fury and thus petrified, we could not help thinking of Pharaoh's desperate pursuit of the Israelites through the foaming waters. The island to our left, looming dimly through the driving snow, was the only land in sight, and we felt that small indeed was our prospect of rescue should the ice, over which we were the first passengers, give way — not, however, that there was much cause to fear such a catastrophe.

Keen blew the blast, and heavily fell the snow, as we proceeded onward along the newly-cut road, with huge slabs of ice piled up on either side of us, on the sharp corners of which an upset would have been far more uncomfortable than our deposit on the snow. Our horses' hoofs sank into the débris of the slabs which the workmen's pickaxes had left, and which looked like thick pieces of frosted glass, and made a clinking noise like it, while the grinding of the runners in it was like the boom of distant waters. As we passed slowly over this bed of smashed ice we likened it to driving through a slate-quarry, while we enjoyed the rolling, jolting, and pitching feeling of being at sea; though the jolting was certainly not to be compared in misery to that inflicted by our old friends the cahots.

Now and then we came to open level spaces, which had frozen out completely only after the surrounding ice had packed, and we could clearly distinguish the slabs which had been floating in the water when the severer frost secured them in their present positions. The danger was, that some of the young ice which encompassed them might not yet be sufficiently strong to bear our weight. To go out of a walk was impossible, so we sat patiently enduring the cold, which was more severe than any we had before encountered; but, fortunately, it was not to continue for any length of time. Speedily my fur coller was encircled with a fringe of snow and icicles, and our hair, and eye-lashes, and eye-brows became frosted over. Right glad were we, therefore, when we could discern the outline of the further shore, and gladder still to climb the bank, and to reach the railway station at St. Lambert's. A heavy stage with four horses crossed after us in safety, so that our friends need not have had any alarm at our undertaking. The clerks and porters at the station were very civil, and we were well pleased to undergo a short delay, while we thawed at the huge stove in the waiting-room, before we entered the "cars," as the railway carriages are as universally called in Canada as they are in America.

The value of Mrs. William Notman's memories is that they give one of the few detailed descriptions of how an old-countrywoman felt when she had to adapt herself to the household ways of Montreal.

She was the wife of William Notman, one of the greatest of Canada's photographers of the nineteenth century. A Scot from Paisley, he came out to Montreal with his wife in 1856, and began the long career as a portrait and scenic photographer which left one of the fullest pictorial records of the city and country.

Mrs. Notman wrote these recollections of 1856 and 1857 some twenty years later, in 1878. They are reproduced here from a copy of her manuscript, lent by her son, the late C. F. Notman, and were first printed in the historical column "All Our Yesterdays" in *The Gazette*, Montreal, May 20, 1946.

My first impression of Canadian domestic life was its plenty and comfort. Everything seemed in such abundance, such piles of lovely apples, such large dishes of honey and preserves, such variety of pies, such nice tea four times a day, no plates of wafers, bread and butter, but good thick honest slices fit for hungry people. Oh how good it all tasted and the hearty welcome with it made it doubly sweet.

Then the self help we saw all around was in a great degree a novel experience — people doing their own work and not beginning to try to do it sub rosa, but with a comfortable content that it was well done as no one could do it for you. Then to see the head of the house going to market and carrying home a basket of provisions as a matter of course, and in those days even young ladies felt able to carry home a pair of gloves or a necktie.

We remained nearly three weeks with these kind friends while our house was approaching completion, and unspeakably valuable to me have been ever since the lessons I daily humbly learned, lessons of incalculable use in the busy life that lay before me, while under that hospitable roof, while the friendships formed have lasted ever since.

It was on the 2nd of November I arrived in Montreal and as the winter set in early that year, we had an early experience of Canadian cold. I own to feeling in my inmost heart a little dismayed at the prospect, thinking it must be something terrible if these precautions I saw going on around me were really necessary, not only putting up double windows but carefully stuffing up every little crevice by which the fresh air could enter. We found at first the stove heat very trying and often during that first winter I felt we were suffering far more from heat than cold.

We were very busy preparing for housekeeping, greatly helped by the experience of our friends, who took pleasure in showing us the best way of setting to work. We found furniture very much cheaper than in the Old Country. Of course it was of another style, lacking the solidity meant to endure for a generation, but it was light and pretty and answered our purpose. Crockery seemed very costly and that generally in use awfully heavy and clumsy.

However, by the 1st of December our nest was ready, and coming to take possession that Saturday night, we had our first sleigh drive and felt the merry tinkle of the bells were welcoming us to our new Canadian home. It seemed strange to find everything in so short a time completely covered by the snow. I could scarcely believe we were to see those strange looking wooden pavements no more till spring.

Of course it took a little time after we had begun housekeeping to get used to the new state of things. The stoves I found a little puzzling and more than all else it took some time to remember the contents of the larder were in a congealed state and to take precautions in time. The markets, of course, were very interesting and strange to newcomers, and it struck one as unspeakably odd to see the poor pigs in the last degree of stiffness standing about — it seemed to us, here and there and everywhere.

In those days a little money went a long way at the market — mutton was very cheap, fowls, good ones, 40¢ a couple; chickens, 2 for 25¢! I remember paying 3½¢ lb. for a fine qtr. beef, and everything was in proportion.

Labor also was cheap. You paid your charwoman about half what you do now.

I was struck by the air of perfectly civil self-assertion and equality of the working classes, so different from what one had been used to. I remember the odd feeling when I heard a butterwoman ask at the door if the woman of the house needed anything, and was rather quenched by the way an old Irishman at work in the cellar accepted a bowl of tea as if he took it to oblige me.

There have been many and great changes in all the streets in these 22 years. There was then a Fire Station at the corner of Bleury and Craig Sts. and it seems as if that terrible bell rang its warning of fire sometimes two or three times in a night, at all events very much more frequently than now.

The Church of the Gesu was not then built and one found it a dismal walk from St. Catherine to Sherbrooke street up Bleury, especially at night, there were so few houses. Of course it has only been of late years that there have been shops in St. Catherine St. West. . . .

Of course there was a more provincial air about everything, far less of a city. The difference was then very marked between the New York and Boston stores. There are few things now one cannot get as well here.

6

Prosperity, Pomp and Plumbing

Samuel Phillips Day was a visitor to Montreal with a particular interest in its industries; in this respect he was unusual, for most visitors were preoccupied with the picturesque. Though Montreal's picturesqueness did not escape his notice, he found himself "pleasingly astonished" to see "factories clustered together" along the banks of the Lachine Canal. To some of these factories he "performed a daily pilgrimage." Being of a practical turn of mind, he recorded in detail what he observed.

Montreal had comparatively little manufacturing before the second half of the nineteenth century. There were, of course, notable exceptions, such as Molson's Brewery, established as far back as the eighteenth century, and the Eagle Foundry, already flourishing by the eighteen-thirties. But in general the city had been concerned with the more spectacular profits to be made in the fur trade, and, later, as an exchange centre for the products of the new settlers to the west and the manufactured goods of the United Kingdom.

The transition to manufacturing became conspicuous about the middle of the century for two reasons. First, the increasing population in and around Montreal and to the west was creating an attractive domestic market; and, secondly, the widening of the Lachine Canal and the installation of the greater locks provided the essential of industry — water-power. The Government leased to industries the land along the canal, and the canal banks became, as Day saw, the clustering place of factories. (When he refers to the "Province" and the "Provincial Government" he is, of course, referring to the Province of Canada, comprising what are now Ontario and Quebec, and to its united Government.)

S. P. Day had a style suited to his purpose; it was clear, matter-of-fact, accurate. He was an Englishman who was a correspondent for the London *Herald* from 1863-4, and for the *Morning Post* in 1865. His visit to Montreal took place in the summer of 1862. This account of the factories along the Lachine Canal appears on pages 179-80, 185-87, 190-2 of volume one of his book *English America: or Pictures of Canadian Places and People* (London, 1864).

The manufacturers of a city or country, no less than their ordinary commerce, must be viewed as so many elements of prosperity and material wealth. I reiterate that those of Montreal surprised me much. I was not prepared for the discovery I had made. Within the past five or six years, or even a briefer period, a variety of manufacturing resources have been developed. Along the banks of the Lachine Canal — the basin of which is two hundred and fifty feet wide — factories and mills are closely congregated; the machinery of each being altogether worked by means of water-power. One leading feature of these establishments is, that machinery is made to do what in the old country is accomplished by human hand. In Canada labour of this description is scarce; and hence, ingenuity or necessity, which we are told is the "mother of invention" has been exercised to beneficial purpose.

Having been supplied with letters of introduction to the principal manufacturers and mill proprietors, I eagerly set about visiting the prominent objects of interest. The first manufactory to which I wended my way was the Victoria Iron Works (the reader will observe how loyal the people are), where I noticed a rolling-mill for nail plates in operation, specimens of which article had been sent to the late International Exhibition. This mill turns out twelve tons per day, chiefly from Scotch pig iron, puddled at the works. One hundred and twenty hands are employed, and two thousand tons of plates were produced during the working months of 1862. The works were commenced as recently as 1859, and, I believe, were the first of the kind started in the Province. There is another rolling-mill in the suburbs of the city, and two nail and spike factories, in one of which I lost my hearing for some minutes, owing to the deafening clamour of the heavy cutting machines — fully a dozen of them being simultaneously in operation. . . .

There are three immense flour mills at Montreal, called the Royal, the City, and the Canal Mills, through the first of which I was politely conducted by one of the proprietors. These structures are not so extensive as the great flour mills of Richmond, Virginia, which I had seen the year before; nevertheless they are very capacious, and possess peculiar features of novelty. The warehouse portion of the Royal Mills is one hundred feet in height by seventy-five feet wide. It has a frontage of one hundred and sixty feet, while the milling department is sixty-five feet square and seventy feet in elevation. The building has eight stories, and from the gravelled flat roof a fine view is had of the busy city and the St. Lawrence. These mills contain forty-four grain bins, having a depth of from twenty-four to thirty-six feet, while the capacity of the warehouse exceeds two hundred thousand bushels. The grinding capacity of the mills is reckoned at eight runs a stone; there are four millstones, and every two make what is called "a run." Five hundred barrels of wheat can be ground daily with ease. The most remarkable feature about these mills is the introduction of "elevators," by means of which a wonderful economy of human labour is realised. The elevators are worked by water-power and remove grain from vessels to the bins. One was in operation during my visit, and I was surprised to find that, while grain was being taken from a barge in the Canal up into the warehouse and weighed, it was transhipped into another vessel lying alongside. By means of elevators a barge could be loaded or unloaded in an hour; a process that would otherwise occupy an entire day, even with the assistance of a large number of hands. There is a "barrel elevator" in the mills for the purpose of raising barrels from one story to another. Even the very barrels are filled and weighed by means of machinery. The complicated and varied work of the Royal Mills is accomplished by the aid of twenty men and boys — an economisation of labour truly wonderful. The proprietors are Englishmen. The grandfather of one served in the British army, and he himself fought in the Rebellion — a true Loyalist I will be bound.

Among the objects of interest are the Canada Marine Works, covering fifteen acres of ground, upon which are erected a foundry, boiler, and finishing shop supplied with all kinds of modern tools. The machinery is driven by a condensing steam engine, besides a large sawing and planing mill worked by steam-power. A considerable portion of the ground is employed as a shipyard, containing two basins, each five hundred feet by one hundred feet in extent. This property was purchased by the present proprietor about seventeen years ago. From 1845 to the autumn of 1862 inclusive, ninety-four vessels were built and launched from this yard. These were principally constructed for the lake and river navigation; the models combining the highest speed with the greatest carrying capacity on a light draught of water. . . .

The Sugar Refinery is likewise an object of interest. It commenced work in January, 1855, and had, accordingly, been in operation seven years. About seven-eighths of the white sugar consumed in the Province are produced here; the remainder being imported from various countries when the price happens to fall a little lower than the current value of that article in Montreal. The capacity of the works is equal to the requirements of Upper and Lower Canada for several years to come; that is if immigration does not set in very rapidly. The great difficulty experienced consists in the extremely limited market that the country affords for refined sugar. For this reason the manufacture of the commodity is discontinued during two or three months every year. The quantity of raw sugar consumed in Canada is estimated at about seven thousand tons annually; the product being white and yellow sugar, and a moderate quantity of syrup. The refinery establishment of Messrs. Redpath and Co. is very complete, being replete with every modern improvement. The building — which is extensive — machinery, etc., cost fifty thousand pounds, while an equal amount of capital is employed in carrying on the business. The animal charcoal required in the manufacture is made on the premises, the gas from the bones being used to light the same. But I must say no more of this head, lest perchance I should be the innocent means of creating in the reader a disgust for refined sugar.

In addition to the factories enumerated there are several others that I had not leisure to inspect, such as the Steam Saw Mills, the Oil and Colour Works, the Candle Works, the Chemical and India Rubber Works, and an immense establishment for the manufacture of doors, window-frames, etc., by means of water-power. The existence of such places is indicative of the energetic character of the people and of the growth and wealth of the city.

To the facilities afforded by the construction of the Lachine Canal, all those results I have been describing must, of course, be attributed. This Canal was executed by the Provincial Government at a cost of two millions of dollars; but the pecuniary benefits that have, and will arise from this outlay, are beyond computation. Not only has it enabled vessels to pass the Lachine rapids, but it has afforded manufacturing facilities equivalent to at least four million horse-power. It has, in fact, revolutionised primitive ideas, so that where the tottering wind-mill once stood is now erected imposing water-works, built strongly enough to last for ages. To the same cause may likewise be traced the material and commercial prosperity of Montreal itself, which this Canal and the works upon its banks have converted into the grand trading and manufacturing centre of the Province.

What it was like for a boy to be brought up in Montreal when it was one of the garrison towns of the British Empire has been described by Fred T. Claxton. The garrison period lasted through almost the first three-quarters of the century. It was a period of colour, vividness and swagger, such as the workaday soldiers of the militia regiments could scarcely replace when the imperial garrison was withdrawn in 1870.

Fred T. Claxton added other recollections of Montreal at that period: recollections of fire-horses, snow-piles, toll-gates, and the visit of Tom Thumb.

Fred T. Claxton was the son of T. James Claxton and entered his father's firm of manufacturers' agents and importers. He was the uncle of the Honourable Brooke Claxton, Canada's Minister of National Defence 1946-54, and the first chairman of the Canada Council. These reminiscences, written in old age when he had retired to San Francisco, appeared in *The Gazette*, Montreal, May 2, May 22 and June 29, 1935.

Numerous regiments were stationed in Montreal, and I recall the 78th Highlanders, 60th Rifles, and a Regiment of Artillery. Standing outside the old High School, corner of University and Dorchester, I saw the artillery swing around Beaver Hall into Dorchester. There had been a heavy fall of snow, and the men wore moccasins, and had wide, short snowshoes slung on their backs. They wore long, Oxford grey greatcoats, black seal wedge-shaped caps, with a red sack on one side. They were probably a thousand strong, marching in fours. After passing St. James Club, they halted opposite the property of the late Harrison Stevens [Stephens]. Then they were commanded to strap on snowshoes, and then off they went along Dorchester St., the shoes making a click-click noise as they hit. It was a sight to see a Regiment on snowshoes, I never had before. After they passed, there was no need for snowplough; the street was smooth.

The 78th Highlanders used to attend Christ Church Cathedral. Swinging around Phillips Place and Phillips Square headed by their band and pipes, they debouched into St. Catherine st., and into the grand old Cathedral. The band went in last, marched right up to the pulpit,

A spring flood of the eighteen-eighties as seen on Notre Dame Street, at the beginning of Chaboillez Square.

Notman Collection, McCord Museum, McGill University

The Ice Palace in Dominion Square in 1889. Storming the Ice Palace at night was the grand climax of the Winter Carnival.

The Tandem Club on one of its Saturday afternoon drives around Mount Royal with sleighs such as only St. Petersburg could rival.

*F. B. Schell's drawing in
"Picturesque Canada," 1882*

Notre Dame Church in Place d'Armes, as seen looking down
St. Urbain Street in winter.

and deposited their drums in pyramid shape, with brasses standing against the drums. When all were seated, it was a wonderful sight to look from the south door along the main aisle. At the end of each pew was a pile of bearskins, ending at the pulpit with the pile of band instruments. If you have never heard a thousand soldiers singing hymns, you have something to hear. Collecting "soldiers" buttons was among the fads of the boys in those days. "Give me a button, soldier," being the common greeting to men off duty. There was a band stand on McGill Campus on the east side of the avenue, where bands of the various regiments gave afternoon concerts for the benefit of the nurses and children who thronged there. I remember when the 60th Rifles had been ordered "Home," the band played and men sang "Sooner or later the time will come when closest friends must say farewell, farewell — farewell — a long farewell." There were many of those present who realized what was meant.

Saturday afternoon was always a day for sports. The men of the regiment held foot races on Sherbrooke Street. Starting at the corner of Union Ave., it was a measured mile to the nearest of the "Towers," with the quarter at McGill College gates, and the half at the John Redpath gate.

There would be a great crowd of soldiers to see their men run, which they did in approved sporting attire, (as little as possible). Judges went ahead and followed the racers in sleighs, and another crowd were at the "Towers" to meet the racers. Sherbrooke Street was also the scene of many a "brush" between lovers of horse flesh. Seated in light cutters, behind fast trotters, with heads stretched out, some with long strides, others with short, rapid strides, they would rush for half a mile or so, and then drive alongside one another and argue the race over again. . . .

There was one young officer who had a team of Esquimaux dogs and sled. He would jump off the sled, run up alongside some dog who was not pulling, give him a lash with his whip, and then, as the sled passed, jumped on again. . . .

Back in the 1860's my father lived on the corner of St. Catherine and University streets, where Eaton's now stands, and where we used to hear the clang of the Cathedral bell when striking the hours, and also when striking the number of a fire alarm box. Everyone knew where a fire was by counting the strokes of the bell and referring to their pocket memorandums of the numbers and locations.

The days of small things, No. 5 station was on the south side of St. Catharine, between Alexander and Bleury streets. There was a hose reel (no engine), a large puncheon on wheels for street watering, a splendid black horse named "Charley," and three or four men. In between fires "Charley" was off in the neighborhood hauling the watering cart. He might be on Sherbrooke or Victoria or Union avenue, but as soon as the first stroke of the Cathedral bell said "Fire," Charley hauled the water cart to the curb, off jumped his driver, unhitched the traces and flung them across Charley's back, pulled the pins from the shaft and jumped on Charley's back. He needed no urging and knew where to go. Off he would gallop straight for the engine house, where the other men were waiting; around he swung and backed into the shafts; two men jumped on the driving seat and the two others were on the footboard, and away they went; no whip was needed, and at a gallop they made their way to the fire. Of course, that system lost valuable minutes, but Montreal was credited with having a very efficient brigade. . . .

About 1864, Montreal was visited by General and Mrs. Tom Thumb under the auspices of that prince of showmen P. T. Barnum. Their performances were held in Nordheimer's Hall, which stood on the north side of St. James street, between Morgan's corner and St. Peter street.

Tom Thumb was 3 feet 2 inches at thirty, and his wife 2 feet 8 inches at 20 years of age. There were always three or four boys and girls invited to the stage to stand beside the midgets for comparison in heights, and I was among the number the day I was there, dressed in the kilt. Of course I was a head taller than the General. They had the daintiest coach and equipment I have ever seen. It was patterned after one of the royal coaches of England. On the box sat a coachman in a wig and cocked hat, while on the footboard was a footman, similarly attired. A pair of tiny Shetland ponies were at the pole, and you may be sure that there was a crowd of small boys running alongside through the streets. They had already toured Europe and had been presented to Her Majesty Queen Victoria. . . .

In those days there were primitive arrangements for the removal of the snow from the streets, which accumulated and packed hard. I remember going down St. Peter street at the end of April, and, while the sidewalks were cleared, one could not see the people on the other side of the street. On St. Catherine street, the piles of snow shovelled from the sidewalks on the one side, and from the roadway on the other were ten feet above the sidewalks; passages had to be dug out for the tradesmen to enter through. At every crossing, where the snow was trodden down hard, there would be a dip, which gradually became deeper and deeper, forming what was called a "cahuat" (called by the boys cowholes), and which gave the occupants of sleighs a good jolt. . . .

At all the main arterial roads leading into the city there were toll gates, at which a small fee (sous) was collected, for the maintenance of the roads. A small house was built alongside, where a toll keeper and his wife lived, and opened and shut the gate to let vehicles pass. There was one on Sherbrooke street about where Greene avenue is.

Through most of the nineteenth century, Montreal was noted for its hotels. Some good hotels had been established by the century's second decade, and they improved and multiplied. Montreal early became a tourists' city. Many visitors were coming to North America to view the great experiment in republican democracy in the United States, and they often concluded their tours by crossing the border at Niagara and coming down the St. Lawrence to Montreal. From there they would visit Quebec, then return to Montreal to leave for one of the ports of the United States by way of Lake Champlain.

As the century moved on visitors came to Montreal in numbers for business, and the stream of tourists increased. Many were Americans who came up to Montreal and Quebec to see something different. The Old World look of part of Montreal and most of Quebec gave a taste of Europe to those who could not take the grander tour across the Atlantic. From the middle of the century on, many Americans stayed at Montreal's hotels on their way to and from the popular summer resorts at Metis, Murray Bay, Tadoussac, and Cacouna. The Civil War brought an influx of visitors from both North and South, as Montreal's neutral position was convenient for refuge or espionage.

Till the opening of the Windsor Hotel on Dominion

Square in the eighteen-seventies, no hotel in Montreal could compare with the St. Lawrence Hall. It stood on the north-west corner of St. James and St. François Xavier, and was known throughout the world of travellers for its efficiency and comfort. It reflected the personality of its proprietor and manager, Henry Hogan. He was meant for the profession by temperament, for he was easy and affable, watchful and confidential. He was clean-shaven as to the chin, but cultivated side-whiskers and a curling moustache. He wore pince-nez glasses and a bow tie, and had a way of emphasizing a point in conversation by lifting three fingers of his right hand and gesturing with them.

A description of the St. Lawrence Hall in the stir of the Civil War period was written by an English visitor, George Tuthill Borrett, a Fellow of King's College, Cambridge. Like many British visitors, he had expected to find Montreal rather a seedy town and was surprised that it had so many fine buildings and so splendid a hotel. He wrote his account of his stay at the St. Lawrence Hall in one of a series of letters to his father, which he later had printed in London in 1865 for private circulation, under the title *Letters From Canada and the United States*. This selection is from pages 30-37.

I suppose you will expect me to tell you something about the hotel life of the New World. . . .

Well, I must ask you to imagine a fine handsome house, after the style of the new hotels in London or Paris, with a noble entrance-hall, fronted by a covered arcade, opening upon a wide well-built street. Before the doorway of the hall will be a busy medley of carts, cabs, carriages, and omnibuses in the road, and drivers, porters, passengers, and baggage on the pavement. Inside the door, upon the right, is the reading-room, with the journals in frames upon reading-desks along the walls; and upon the left you will find the bar or coffee-room — a sort of well-dressed English taproom — and all about the doorway, the reading-room, and the bar, you will jostle against a crowd of noisy visitors, and hear such a buzz of human voices, as will drown the turmoil of the traffic in the street. A few steps further in, and you will find yourself in a lofty second or inner hall, where the noise and bustle seems ten times greater than at the entrance to the hotel. Opposite to you, at the further end of this inner hall, will be a long counter, on which lies the visitors' book, with guide-books, maps, almanacks, and directories, and behind the counter you will see the *maître-d'hôtel*, with his cashiers, clerks, and various assistants. On the right of the hall you will find the post office and newspaper-stall, circulating library, and telegraph bureau; and on the left the lavatory and, not the least important, the barber's shop. All along the counter, and in and out the barber's shop you will see and hear the most doing. At the counter, from morning to night, one incessant roll of clamour for beds and bills, and at the barber's from dawn till dinner, a succession of unshorn Yankees — a Yankee never shaves himself — submitting their cheeks to the barber's razor, and their ears to his latest news. You must not mind smoke, for you will be smothered with it; you must learn to tolerate chewing, or you will get bilious; you must be indifferent to spitting, or you will die of nausea. Montreal is crammed with Americans; they are always here in great numbers, and now the war has at least doubled them. Southerners there are some, but Yankees preponderate; and with all the occupants of the hotel, be they of what nation they may, Yankee manners and customs are certainly the fashionable thing. But you must take no notice of these little eccentricities of our funny cousins, and look at the master, the host himself. You will see him smoking his cigar behind the counter, and conversing with his visitors right and

left, exchanging civilities with his new-comers, and shaking
hands with those who are leaving him — very attentive,
very affable; in fact, exactly suited to his work, and this is
saying a great deal, for a formidable task it must be to
manage the details of the various departments in one of
these gigantic establishments, and well may the Yankees
form their estimate of a man's smartness by his natural
capacity for keeping an hotel.

Passing on through the hall, and ascending the grand
staircase, you will reach the reception-room — a handsome
salon, of large and lofty dimensions, with anterooms and
boudoirs attached to it; and here you will find ladies and
gentlemen in knots upon the chairs and sofas, receiving
visitors, or conversing amongst themselves; and at the
piano, in the centre of the room, ten to one but you will
see a precocious young Yankee girl, of the age of sixteen
perhaps, or under, playing away before the assembled
multitude, perfectly regardless of the ears and eyes intent
upon her — possibly even impudent enough to be practising her scales. Further on you will come upon the
dining-hall — an elegant room like the last, entered by
splendidly wide passages or corridors, and filled with innumerable small tables, which hold from four to eight or
ten "covers" each. The bedrooms are large, light, and
airy, and the ventilation of the building perfect.

It is a noisy life this, of course; but for a bachelor
travelling "solo" I can imagine nothing more entertaining, and the living is cheap enough, when compared with
the rates of our first-class hotels at home. Throughout this
continent the charge is always so much per day, on the
principle of the foreign "pensions," and at all the best
hotels in Canada that charge is now two dollars, i.e., some-

thing over eight shillings. For this you get bed, breakfast, luncheon, dinner, tea, and supper — such a meal at each sitting as would feast a Londoner for a week — everything in fact but beverages other than water, or what an American elegantly terms "drinks." Breakfast goes on from 8 to 11, lunch from 1 to 2, dinner from 5 to 7, tea from 8 to 10, supper from 11 to 12, which signifies that to obtain any particular meal you must present yourself at some time between the two hours during which it is announced as obtainable.

Breakfast I think the most striking meal, and so I will ask you to accompany me to that. We will drop in, say at 9.30, sit down casually at any of the numerous tables which has a vacant place, and in a business-like tone of voice call for the carte. . . . I find now that it is all absolutely true, and that a man, who sits down and orders an egg and a bit of toast, has just as much chance of getting any one to wait upon him, as he has of seeing the Thames pure, or the Conservatives in office, or any other physical impossibility.

So we are wise, and instead of selecting such dishes as we wish to try, point out to the waiter some two or three, of the fourteen, which we do not care to venture upon, and boldly order up the rest. The effect upon the waiter is magical; he puts us down as "smart ones," and civility and attention are at once secured. This was my plan on my first breakfast here, but the result of the order was somewhat alarming, for I found myself in about two minutes surrounded by a multitude of little oval dishes, on which were fish, steaks, chops, ham, chicken, turkey, rissoles, potatoes (boiled, roast and fried), cabbage, corn, cheese, onions and pickles, besides plates of hot rolls, buns, crumpets, toast and biscuits, flanked by a great jug full of milk and an enormous vessel of coffee. . . .

Luncheon is served on the same liberal scale, dinner, tea, and supper, ditto. It is no use trying to shirk a dish, the waiters will insist on your trying everything, so your only course is to try. Everybody tries every dish; no one feels any compunction at leaving untouched what has been brought to him; waste is immaterial, for meat is dirt-cheap, vegetables and fruit abundant. All ages of either sex eat extravagantly; no one looks astonished to see "a lovely plant of sixteen summers," tucking down at breakfast kidneys, ham, and sausages after a tremendous plateful of fish; no one stares to see a precocious youth of nine going straight through the dinner carte like a steam mowing-machine, puffing, and blowing, and spitting like an ill-used engine. It is a wonderful thing, truly, this Yankee appetite. I have been told in England that I myself am not deficient in this respect; I admit a considerable executive capacity — but set me down by a middle-aged Yankee lady, and by her side I am a mouse.

Plumbing was slow in developing in Montreal in the nineteenth century. Even in the second half of the century, despite the existence of waterworks, many houses had no direct water supply. In the eighteen-sixties water was still being sold by the bucket from carts in the streets, even as it was described by Mrs. Lovell in the eighteen-thirties.

An analytical description of plumbing in Montreal as he had known it in the eighteen-sixties was given by J. W. Hughes in 1908. Few men could have spoken out of greater knowledge. A Londoner, born in 1845, he had come as a child of four with his parents to Montreal, and was at an early age apprenticed to the plumbing trade in the firm of Richard Patton. Later, as head of his own firm of J. W. Hughes & Son, he became one of the largest contractors for steamfitting and plumbing in Canada.

J. W. Hughes made himself a scientist — almost a philosopher — in plumbing, its practical skills and its role in public sanitation. He wrote many papers on plumbing and hygiene for scientific journals. In 1897 the annual meeting of the American Public Health Association (representing the United States, Mexico and Canada) appointed him chairman of a new committee on drainage, plumbing and ventilation in public and private buildings. He was appointed examining expert in plumbing to the city of Montreal. In 1904 McGill University arranged for him to give a series of twenty-five lectures on plumbing to the students in architecture.

This description of plumbing in Montreal in the eighteen-sixties is reproduced from the extracts of an address, delivered by Hughes in 1908 to the Montreal Architects' Sketch Club, which were published under the title "How Plumbing Was Done in Montreal Fifty Years Ago" by *The Plumber and Steamfitter and Sanitary Engineer of Canada,* Montreal and Toronto, June 1, 1908. The words "fifty years" are used in a general way. The period he describes would appear to be about the year 1865.

It is nearly fifty years since my active interest in matters connected with the building trade began, and during that time many changes in almost all departments of the business have taken place. Plumbing has almost completely changed in men, methods and materials. . . .

As to the changes in methods and materials, I will describe, as nearly as memory will permit, the plumbing of the old-time house of the better class in Montreal, which still stands. The provision for sewage consisted of a cesspool in the yard. This was a large hole in the ground, walled round with rough stones, (sometimes with cedar logs). About three feet below the surface of the ground, cedar logs were laid over the opening, and the earth filled in, occasionally (not always) a manhole was made to give access to the pit for cleaning or observation purposes, but this was rather the exception than the rule, and I have vivid recollections of time spent in trying to find where the cesspool was located, when some derangement of the sewers made it necessary to see what the conditions in the pit were. There was no thought of ventilating the pit; no one knew of any necessity for such a thing. Sewer gas (and there is no such gas known to science) and the microbe had not been discovered, and people were not worrying themselves about what they did not know. Many of these pits gave no trouble; they were known as leaching pits, being built in sandy or gravelly soil, the water disappeared, leaving only the solid matter. Some years ago I had occasion to enter one of these pits that had been in use a great many years, probably fifty, and there was nothing in it except about 6 inches of a fine black earthy matter. When the pit was sunk in hard, or clayey soil, there was trouble from flooding. . . .

The w.c. was enclosed in handsome woodwork, in fact, cabinet work, generally of Spanish mahogany, nicely panelled, and put together with screws, when the architect and plumber could get the carpenter to use them, but there was a standing quarrel between carpenter and plumber on this point, as nails seemed to be the carpenters' pet, and when the plumber had to get the woodwork off to make necessary repairs, the destruction and disfigurement of handsome and expensive woodwork was sometimes pitiable, and the plumber's character still suffers from the reputation he then made as a vandal and destroyer of property. . . .

The wash basins were much the same as at present in use, but we had no oval basins. The slabs were marble, and the woodwork elaborate, the enclosure under the basin being used as a general storage place for all sorts of rubbish. The basin was not separately trapped, the w.c. trap serving for the basin or basins and bath.

The baths were usually of lead, fitted nicely in a wooden box. The lead was put in in two pieces, the body and head being in one piece and the end soldered in. The fittings were the same as now in general use, that is, the standing waste and washer, with the water coming in from the bottom or end, but instead of the fittings being nickled brass, they were made of lead, with brass mountings, the cocks and drop plug being of brass. On top of the woodwork was fitted a nicely engraved plate indicating hot, cold and waste. This form of bath supply and waste was abandoned years ago as being unsanitary, as it certainly is, but has been revived as part of the open plumbing work system, the objection to it being the large surfaces that are not properly flushed and inaccessible for cleaning. The usual panelled woodwork enclosed the bath, and they were frequently fitted with hot and cold showers, made of lead pipe, in a very ornamental manner. . . .

The pantry sinks were of lead, fitted with the usual brass plug and washer; and trapped with the ordinary P. trap. The kitchen sinks were almost invariably of stone. They were generally set in the recess of the basement window, supported on brick piers, with a space left for the trap. It was a nice job for the plumber to wipe in the brass plug washer in the recess left for same in the stone, as if he was not careful in getting up the necessary heat the sink would be split, and they were expensive, being chipped out of a solid piece of native limestone. The sink would be trapped, but why is a mystery, as the waste would be simply dropped into the barrel drain, immediately below it . . .

Having briefly alluded to the waste and soil pipe system, it is now in order to take up the question of the water supply. There was generally two sources from which the water was taken. The well in the yard, for hard water, and a cistern supplied from the house roof gutters and spouts for soft water. These cisterns in the better class of houses were elaborate affairs built of brick and cemented, there being a portion separated from the general cistern by a soft brick partition, through which the water filtered. Beside the sink was set a pump, frequently made of lead. This pump was connected to the suction pipes of the well and cistern so that by opening and shutting the cocks, either hard or soft water could be pumped; from the pump ran a lead rising main up to the cistern, in the attic, or perhaps over the w.c., with a tell-tale pipe from the top of the cistern, water running from which gave the information that the cistern was full.

From the storage cistern was run a water service pipe to supply the different fixtures, and instead of the hot water boiler now in general use, a portion of the cistern was partitioned off, and served as the hot water reservoir, there being two pipes run from it to the range, a flow and return. This portion of the cistern was fitted with a cover; but the general storage cistern was left exposed to what might come along, and sometimes queer things happened. It was not uncommon for rats and mice to be drowned in the tank, and on one occasion on hauling to uncover the soft water tank under the basement floor, my attention was called to some dark object floating on the water. On further investigation it turned out to be the mortal remains of the pet cat that had been missing for some time. . . .

Wood stoves were in universal use and I had been some years at the trade before the introduction of the first coal burners for either heating or cooking. From the kitchen range through a flange in the floor the smoke pipe was run up into the dining room, and on it was fitted a dumb stove. This was a large radiator, through which the smoke passed before it entered the dining room chimney. In the hall stood a box stove capable of taking a three-foot stick of wood. On the top of the stove, was fitted a gallows pipe, another form of radiator of the same class as the dumb stove, but of a different shape. On top of the stove stood the evaporator. Why do we not provide for evaporation now? It is much needed and would make for comfort and economy. After the smoke had passed through the gallows pipe it was carried through pipes along the hall and up through the well of the stairs between the hand-rails, along the upper hall through the front bed-room into the chimney. And there you have the old-time heating apparatus in the ordinary dwelling, many of which still stand. These houses were not uncomfortable, because in their construction great care was taken to keep out the cold.

Imagine what a domestic disturbance it was every spring taking down the stoves and pipes, cleaning them and storing them away in the attic or woodshed. Then in the fall they had to be taken out and refitted. This was the tinsmiths' harvest time — the plumber was a point above that sort of work. He was no tinker in those days. To-day with the hot water furnaces, it is up to the plumber. Just imagine houses, stores, churches, schools, court house, public halls being warmed with stoves on the general lines I have described, but so they were, as I well know, as my first experience was as a tinsmith, and if I am a plumber to-day it is largely owing to my desire to escape the terrible stove-piping of spring and fall. . . .

As far as the ordinary houses were concerned, there was not any special effort made to ventilate the dwellings, except that the hall stove with its roaring fire was a most excellent and effective ventilator. It used up a large quantity of air, and this air had to come in from outside, so the old-timer had a ventilator lacking in the modern house, where the furnace is generally in the cellar.

The masses of the people in my early days in Montreal were not troubled with plumbers' bills, because they had no plumbing in their houses. While there was a waterworks, and certain streets were provided with mains, the introduction of water into the houses was by no means universal, and there were large districts where there were no mains. The water was distributed from barrels drawn on a two-wheeled cart, carried into the house in tin pails of a regulation size, the price being three pails for a penny.

St. Helen's Island in the St. Lawrence opposite Montreal, chosen to be part of the site of the World's Fair (Expo '67) , was a military station through much of the nineteenth century. Its position, from a military point of view, was strategic. Fortified, with batteries, it could prevent an enemy crossing to Montreal from the South Shore, or mounting the river. If it were to fall into an enemy's hands, it could command Montreal, for batteries placed there could easily bombard the city.

Fearing an attack on Montreal from the United States, the British Government bought part of the island from its owners, the Longueuil family, about 1807, and began to erect military buildings. In 1818 the Government acquired the whole island. There a garrison was maintained till the British troops were finally withdrawn in 1870. The island was then ceded to the Government of Canada. The city of Montreal was accorded the use of it as a park in 1874, and finally became its owner, after long negotiations, in 1908.

This fortified island in the river added to the garrison look that Montreal had at this period. A gun on the island was fired at noon, and its battery gave thunderous salutes on royal anniversaries and other important occasions.

But delightful as St. Helen's Island was, heavily wooded and set in the river, the garrison there lived in monotony and boredom, as may be seen in the account by Lieut. Francis Duncan.

Francis Duncan (1836-1888) was an officer of literary tastes. Born at Aberdeen, the eldest son of an advocate, he graduated from Marischal College and entered the Royal Artillery in 1855. He served in British North America from 1857 to 1862. He commanded the Egyptian Artillery from 1883 to 1885, and did much to forward the expedition sent for the relief of General "Chinese" Gordon at Khartoum. In 1885 he reached the rank of colonel in the Army and was made a Companion of the Bath. He was a fluent and lively writer. His books include a *History of the Royal Regiment of Artillery, The English in Spain,* and *The Royal Province of New Scotland and Her Baronets.*

This account of garrison life on St. Helen's Island in 1862 will be found on pages 251-58, 261-62, 265-68, 270-71 of the book he wrote on his military experiences in British North America, *Our Garrisons in the West or Sketches in British North America* (London, 1864).

I wonder if any of my readers ever suffered from the Crusoe mania, a disease which makes one pine to be away in some lone island in the sea, where the only thing to be dreaded would be the print of the human foot, where some intelligent dog or goat should more than compensate for the loss of the human race; where, under the exertions of one's unaided hand, acres of wild ground should become fertile, and damp caves be changed into impregnable fortresses from without, but imperial salons within?

Hear, then, the words of one who dwelt on a lonely island, with the fortress old but ready-made, with a marvellous lack of society, but an aggravating abundance of the beautiful; near to a large city, and yet so far, owing to a rapid river — and then believe me that islands are a delusion, and solitude a snare. How often have I gnashed my teeth, as, meeting some adventurous acquaintance engaged in a pic-nic, I have been greeted with, "What! *you* living here! Oh, how charming you must find it! So picturesque, so quiet, so lovely!" At these moments lunacy became imminent, and the melancholy which, from hopelessness of sympathy, I was obliged to conceal, became a devouring fiend.

Our island was small, uncommonly small, so confoundedly small that, including every stone and promontory in its whole circumference, we could accomplish its circuit in half an hour; and our constitutional walks must have averaged generally ten or twenty per diem. For I have always observed in my life that the more restricted our opportunities are for gratifying a propensity, the more methodical and determined are we in carrying it out, and the more positive we are in maintaining the necessity of this gratification. . . .

We came to regard our island much as that unhappy polar bear in the Regent's Park Zoological Gardens must view the few wet slabs on which it walks up and down, sometimes forwards, sometimes backwards, now wagging its head solemnly, now bowing ridiculously, yet all the while affecting to think that it had the whole unlimited use of the Arctic regions, but failing horribly in the attempt. To make matters worse, our island was in a river, not in stationary water — a river with a rapid current and mighty volume — no less a river than the great St. Lawrence. The wind blew this river into ugly waves at times, and cut us, with our little skiffs, off from the mainland; and, even in calm weather, the weary current so prolonged the labour of crossing, that after achieving the feat one always felt inclined never to re-attempt it.

Our island is situated opposite Montreal, the commercial capital of Canada, and is surrounded on other sides by the fertile plains of St. Lambert, St. Hyacinth, and La Prairie. It is a military station only, and to civilians landing the stern warning is given that martial law is to be obeyed. Oh, merry paradox, and strange picture of peace and war! where the guns are strewn thickest, the grass is greenest and the wild flowers fairest; where tons and tons of powder lie buried in a dark magazine, the frogs croak loudest in my ears as I visit the lonely post at night, and the wild strawberry blushes under my feet, and the elms wave greenly over my head. My sword, as I do my rounds, clanks not heavily on paved parades, nor echoes ringingly in the ears of armed men; it drags lightly over the green moss, and rings only against some fallen trees or flower-buried stone. In Dickens's "Bleak House" the sketch of Mr. Boythorn raging and storming with the canary perched on his head is not more ludicrous — ay, even to the pathetic — than the picture which I see every day. The birds perched on the top of order-boards, hanging on silent walls, but breathing the sternest denunciations against possible offenders; while the spider, weaving its web on a summer day across the door of a vacant sentry-box, is no inappropriate companion to the martins that build their nests amid the pile of shot and shell, and feed their young in the shadow of cannon and other instruments of war. . . .

It had a ludicrous idea that it was fortified, had our island. There was a decayed and trembling drawbridge, and in various parts of the island were the remnants of what may once have been formidable gates, but whose rheumatic bars were now swayed about, creaking and groaning, by every summer breeze. Under my window was a platform, once meant to support a gun, but which was now past supporting itself. From under its rotting timbers one day I heard a sound, by no means unfamiliar, but hardly warlike, and presently out strutted a stately fowl, accompanied by a brood of newly-hatched chickens, whose chirping seemed a satire on the heavy boom meant to echo amid the dense smoke hanging over the gun whose existence never went beyond some sanguine fancy. . . .

To further gloom in our minds we had a cemetery on our island, where, according to the rude wooden tombstones, the victims to a plague which once broke out on the island were huddled in unseemly crowd: prisoners in their lives, in their deaths they were not released. It was situated in a gloomy recess, where the snow lay longest, and the sunbeams could not penetrate; where the grass was rank and weedy, and your feet went splashing through green and hidden pools, while the white tombstones stood out in the uncertain light like ghosts.

For anachronisms we had our block-houses, our gates, and our guard-rooms. On the tops of imposing rocks were to be seen dark windowless buildings buried in a rank undergrowth of shrubs, towers whose dismal walls whisper of death and defiance; but ah! when we come near them, like many men whom we meet in life, we detect the

cracked roof, the rotting rafters, and read in their linea-
ments weakness and imbecility.

And our gates, what gates so fearful in aspect, what
spikes more likely to make the human frame shiver, till a
nearer inspection shows the broken lock and missing
hinge, and some summer breeze comes and shakes their
creaking ribs in ribaldry, like rheumatism and palsy playing antics with a cripple's bones. And our guard-rooms —
one there is on the quiet beach of the quietest part of our
island, where adventurous cows wander in utter amaze-
ment, where solemn pigs grunt, and vain fowls cackle —
half, merely, of a house whose other half is tenanted by
an ancient dame whose life is spent in washing linen,
which, in the form of nameless garments, flaps in the very
face of our bearded guard. Ah! this, our guard-room, is
the climax of our paradox, and here we sit down and
laugh. For seizing an hour for rest from her steaming toil,
our ancient dame sits down on the rickety seat before the
guard-room door, and laughs with the men as if they were
but children playing at some solemn game, while the
fowls pick seeds from under the butts of their carbines,
and the wild duck comes close in to the shore as if it
knew they were not loaded; and the clank of their swords
as they saunter up and down mingles with the drowzy
hum of grasshoppers, or the whisperings of the trees.

And our island had its ghost, in a dark frog-haunted
pool near our largest magazine, in a lonely part of the
island, the solitary sentry has been known to see rise in
the still watches of the night a green lady whose chief
amusement was to scream — a hysterical ghost whose fit
never wore off.

The only other inhabitants were a few old pensioners,

encouraged to live there no doubt by an economical government with the object of accelerating their end and of shortening their pensions. Inasmuch as we were wholly dependent on these individuals for the produce of the cow and the domestic fowl, we did not object to the arrangement. A few transitory individuals in the form of infantry come over for musketry instruction were never regarded by us as part of the community; indeed, living as they did under canvas and being engaged the whole day, we would hardly have been aware of their existence were it not that their firing often closed one angle of "our island" against our daily constitutionals. . . .

A month or two on the island rendered us all very dyspeptic; and dyspepsia rendered us miserably uncertain in our tempers. We would part in cheerful and jovial mood, say at ten o'clock: at eleven we would meet taciturn and scowling; on parade we would study the countenance of our commanding officer as he came on, with feelings akin to those of a dog walking on tip-toe round a strange and larger dog; mingled feelings of awe, interest, and uncertainty. Did his face look bright and his eyes clear — we also at once looked bright and felt relieved. Did the skin look muddy, the eye yellow, the general appearance bilious, then we looked for squalls. For myself, I look back with disgust to the cynical and misanthropic brute which my residence on that island made me. Practising at cricket, if anyone made a hit which necessitated my running for it, I scowled at and hated that man with a murderous hatred. Our once placid rubber [of whist] became vicious as any old ladies' at Bath; we criticised our food until the cook must frequently have contemplated suicide in despair; we even gave up corresponding much with our friends in the outer world, partly, indeed, because we had nothing to say, but partly also because in our bosoms the milk of human kindness, that lifeblood of the domestic affections, had turned to gall. We had our moods pensive, and moods merry, verging even on hysterics; the former I associate chiefly in my mind with sherry cobblers, the latter with unlimited claret-cup. . . .

But the most melancholy feature in our imprisonment was the woful lack of energy and application which supervened. Two of my brother officers contemplated writing a treatise on some such subject as Napoleon I., and agreed to divide the labour in rather a novel manner; one doing the reading, the other the writing. They failed to get beyond the first chapter, and ended as most of our enterprises did — in beer.

In an effervescing fit of zeal, we all agreed one day to go in for water-colours. Rushing over to Montreal we purchased the materials, hunted up and down the streets for a master, engaged him to come over regularly for purposes of instruction; got through our first lesson, yawned through our second, and on the morning of the third sent him a message that on that day we were engaged. His periodical visits coming round on us, made us soon regard him as another Old Man of the Sea; nor could we find any way or excuse for getting rid of him, for he was an excellent artist and a tolerable teacher, nor could we plead no further need of his services. At last, one day, there came a rumour that we were to be removed to Quebec; so meeting in solemn conclave, we concocted an elaborate letter to him, stating that our preparations for departure were so urgent, our setting our house in order so engrossing, that we feared we could not give that attention to his valuable instructions which they merited, and therefore, &c. &c.

We attempted fishing from our island, and occasionally caught some of the most diminutive fish that ever existed, provided, with what seemed to us, a most unnecessary abundance of bones. Duck-shooting was attempted; but further than a great amount of discomfort incurred, and firing off our guns on our return, we can hardly be said to have had much excitement from this sport.

Shut out as we were from the world, I remember, as in a dream, that we were always craving for news. The post came over twice a day, and we generally went down in a body to meet him, and lived in constant expectation of letters. Every time any of our number crossed to Montreal he was received with yells of execration if he dared to return without some intelligence. Fortunately, the very air in America, that year, was rife with rumours, and our morbid and almost Yankee anxiety for news was generally gratified abundantly. As for the little events that occurred in our own community, they furnished us with as much conversation as any choice tit-bits of scandal would an old lady's tea-table in a country village. An occasional desertion (I wonder every one did not desert), sickness, an exchange, or any small matter, was long and well-ventilated. Our man, I remember, disappeared one night, and after a considerable lapse of time his body was brought up from the muddy bottom of the river by the dredging-machine. The chatter about this was childish; and though the man had not been overpopular in his life, yet all were anxious to go to his funeral for a new sensation.

I had almost forgot to mention, among other enterprises which we undertook with spasmodic energy — that we seriously contemplated a heavy course of gardening. An acre of land, or so, near our quarters, had once been cultivated for potatoes. On this we cast covetous eyes, and soon obtained authority to appropriate it. A solemn commission was sent into Montreal to purchase seed, tools, flower-pots, and frames, sufficient altogether to start in life, with the greatest comfort, several market-gardeners. Before the purchased goods reached us, the fit had worn off; and with the exception of one small bed of salad, on which, while yet in infancy, many cows danced one frenzied night, the acre or so remained Bareacres the whole summer. . . .

But to our cloud there was a silver lining. There was one thing of which we never wearied. At night, on the shore or on the green parapet, to stand watching the play of the merry stars on that hurrying river, or the grand white sheen of the patient moon spreading over its surface like a garment. Shadows on the shore, light on the water and in the tree-tops, a great silence everywhere — one never wearied then. The buzz of some lazy insect, or the echo of distant oars on the St. Lawrence, with the cry, at stated intervals, of "All's well" from the sentry on his lonely post under the elms by the haunted pool, these were the only sounds that broke the sweet stillness of that moonlight, and made it seem stiller and sweeter. So might one dream for ever in that happier land where the Lord himself shall lighten all things, and the nations of them that are saved shall dwell in the light of it!

And as one would stand gazing, he would see the many lights of a great city come twinkling over the rippling water as if to cheer without interrupting one's solitude. Or one might hear, borne fitfully on the night-air, the bells of many churches sounding each passing hour, or inviting one to pray in a voice more solemn in this still island than in the crowded streets and thronging populace of a restless city. . . .

And at last we left our island. On a bright September day a small steamer came and carried us away to put us on our first stage to England. We were marched on board with hardly energy enough to cheer; and we babbled in an idiotic manner to one another. We could not realize that we were actually going, that the speck on the horizon, getting smaller and smaller, was our island, fading from our sight for ever. And in the wild nights at sea, its image rose before our minds in a strange and unearthly calm, such as one could fancy to a man awakened from a trance, must the dim, mysterious gap in his life appear. And then, months after, came the first letter I received from one of our successors on the island. It seemed so strange to hold that thin sheet of paper in my hand and to think that the words had been written by the drowsy trees and scorching grass I knew so well. Instinctively it all came before me like a dream — the grey barracks, the dark pool, the little yard of the silent, the hot air, the surging river. And like the forgiveness of injuries, when those who did them are dead, so did this, our island, seem more endurable now, when far away from its dreary paths, its melancholy shores.

Mark Twain, in Montreal in 1881, said: "This is the first time I was ever in a city where you couldn't throw a brick without breaking a church window."

Certainly Montreal, especially in Victorian days, was a city of churches. Mrs. Harriet Beecher Stowe, on her visit in 1869, put it in these words: "Montreal is a most religious city. . . . Montreal is a mountain of churches." But as churches were what interested her most in any city, she prepared to enjoy Montreal.

It was as a religious crusader that she had written *Uncle Tom's Cabin*, believing that its inspiration was coming from God. The book had been a power in the Civil War, and its message of freedom spread round the world, translated into twenty-three languages.

Not only did this "diminutive mother, shabby, life-worn, looking older than her years," believe herself to be the instrument of God; her family abounded in clergymen. Her father was a theologian; her husband was a teacher in a theological college; and her brother, Henry Ward Beecher, was probably the most popular preacher in the United States.

In her room in the Ottawa Hotel on St. James Street she turned to the newspaper advertisements of the churches and made her selection. In the morning she went to the little Church of St. John the Evangelist, then at the corner of Dorchester and St. Urbain Streets, where Father Edmund Wood was introducing "high," or ritualistic, practices into the diocese, amidst controversy and ridicule. The courage of unpopular convictions had a natural appeal to the author of *Uncle Tom's Cabin*.

She says she went in the afternoon to the "Scotch Presbyterian Church." This was presumably the Scotch Presbyterian Church on St. Gabriel Street, the historic old fieldstone building erected in 1792 on land granted by the Government from the west end of the Champ de Mars, where the westward extension of the Old Court-house stands today. She speaks of the sermon by a well-known Montreal preacher, "the Rev. Mr. Frazer." This may have been the Reverend Joshua Fraser, the minister of St. Matthew's Presbyterian Church. In the evening she went to hear the son of the Marquis of Exeter preach as a Plymouth Brother.

Mrs. Stowe's account of her visit to Montreal appeared in the magazine *Hearth and Home*, and was reproduced in the *Evening Telegraph and Daily Commercial Advertiser*, Montreal, June 1, 1869.

. . . Montreal is a mountain of churches. Every shade and form of faith is here well represented in wood or stone, and the gospel feast set forth in every form and shape to suit the spiritual appetite of all inquirers.

A long list of newspaper advertisements in the Saturday evening papers sets forth such an amount of preaching and praying in various places on Sunday, that the stranger is puzzled with the variety.

At daybreak on Sunday morning a loud chorus of bells announced to the world that it was Whit Sunday, or, as our Catholic brethern call it, Pentecost.

We had choice of many churches, but on the principle of seeking out the sect that is everywhere spoken against, we chose a small Ritualistic church on a narrow, obscure street which is repudiated by the Church and ridiculed by the world, who give it the designation of "Wood's Minstrels." Here we found, however, a crowded congregation of serious, earnest people, who sung the ordinary English Service of the Book of Common Prayer, instead of saying it. Now, as the Rubric expressly provides that it shall be said or sung, it is hard to see what departure from order there is in that.

The music used was the Gregorian tunes, and every man, woman, and child in the church stood up and joined heartily and with one accord, and looked so serious and earnest that we could not but ask whether it would be any better or more acceptable to God if they had sat in dozing quietude while a quartette choir in a distant part of the church performed their praises and prayers for them in the most select opera airs of the season. Such are the practices that we remember in many churches where the praises of God are entirely given over into the hands of three or four paid artists. The sermon was very short, very earnest, very simple and scriptural, and although entirely without any ambition or effort at rhetorical or logical power, had much that might edify a simple Christian. There were one or two expressions which we could have wished different, which struck us as unwise, but, on the whole, the spirit of the whole was refreshingly earnest and devout.

Would it not be better if those who spend their breath in scolding about the ritualistic movement would, in place of this, imitate certain points in their service — their energy, their whole-hearted devotion? If each party, instead of abusing the other, would study and endeavor to adopt each other's really useful and strong points, would not the Church and the world both be improved?

In the afternoon, the Rev. Mr. Frazer preached in the Scotch Presbyterian church. Here, too, was a crowded, serious, earnest congregation, and here, too, was congregational singing from the old Scotch version, the whole congregation standing up and singing the good old tune of Lennox with a loud voice, in a refreshing manner. Mr. Frazer is a zealous preacher, of the style that we should call Revivalist in the States, and is, we perceive, very widely known and appreciated here. In the evening, that we might go to the extreme end of the pole, we went to a private hall to hear Lord A. P. Cecil, the son of the Marquis of Exeter, a Plymouth brother, who threw up his commission of officer in the British army that he might devote himeslf to the work of a missionary in the wilds of Canada.

At the appointed hour, we saw upon the platform a tall, slender young man, of about five and twenty, well formed, lithe and elastic in his figure, with a finely turned head, rather delicate and classical features, with small white hands, and an appearance betokening breeding and refinement. He was dressed in a simple grey suit, and had a small testament and hymn-book.

He began by reading the first verse of a revival hymn, which he then sung, and was joined in it by the whole audience. He then knelt down and prayed with an impassioned earnest simplicity that was quite touching. After this he opened his testament and began the exposition of Luke 15. His audience seemed to be mostly composed of plain, earnest people, of the middle and working classes, who had come with testaments provided, which they also opened and followed him.

The principle characteristic of his preaching was a fervent, earnest simplicity and an undoubting faith. FAITH — simple, literal faith in the words of Jesus, seemed to be the whole of his message. It was a pointing to the personal, present Jesus, and a plea with every soul to embrace him as a Saviour.

When we returned late in the evening to our hotel, our waiter appeared to suppose that of course we had been attending the preaching at the church of the Jesuits, and seemed so sincerely to lament that we had missed it, and gave such glowing accounts of what we should have heard, that we were quite obliged to him. Thus earnestly, in so many ways in this cold, intense, earnest Canada, is the One Great Concern pressed upon our attention.

For ourselves, we listened to one and all with no desire to criticise. . . .

In our very neighborhood, the wondrous sound of the great bells of Notre Dame tell us of services going on there, which doubtless bring peace to many pious souls who have been led by the ancient pathways of Rome.

The services there are not to us intelligible, but we do not the less appreciate what they may be to those differently educated. The schools, hospitals, works of charity of the Romish Church here, are something immense, and we should not envy the heart of that person who could pass through them all without a thrill of sympathy and a wishing of God-speed to these workers for human good.

7

Pageantry, Problems and Pleasures

The scope the celebration of St. Jean Baptiste Day had reached is impressively seen by 1870. The society had been founded in Montreal in 1834 by Ludger Duvernay, primarily to defend and promote the institutions and language of the French-Canadian people. At first it tended toward political radicalism, and many of those who participated in its founding became involved in the Rebellion of 1837-38. These disturbances and their aftermath delayed the progress of the society, and it did not become operative in Montreal till 1843. At first there was some indifference. But it soon expanded with the solid backing of the Roman Catholic Church, which brought it under its influence.

This account of the celebrations of 1870 is of interest as showing how deeply the society had become devoted to the concept that the survival of the French-Canadian people depended on their clinging to the soil and continuing to be farmers. The sermon preached in Notre Dame Church, after the procession had entered, warned against abandoning the farms and losing touch with the soil. It is remarkable that such a sermon should have been preached to a gathering of city-dwellers.

But it continued to be the theme of the St. Jean Baptiste Society in Montreal, as may be seen by comparing it with the address delivered by H. Giraux at the fiftieth anniversary gathering of the society in 1884. He also warned the people against the soul-killing life of the cities. "Farming gives birth to security," he said, "its work ennobles man. How very different is the money-grubbing toil of the factories. The cultivation of the soil is a prayer which is carried to Heaven on the wings of the breeze. . . . "

This is the "pastoral ideal" which became the "pastoral myth"; for, as the Royal Commission on Bilingualism and Biculturalism pointed out in 1965 in its first report, the proportion of the Quebec population living on farms has fallen lower than the average in Canada.

This account of the St. Jean Baptiste procession, when the Papal Zouaves were featured, is translated from the report in *La Minerve*, Montreal, June 25, 1870.

In many streets no effort was spared to make the decorations superb. On all sides waved the flags, mingling the maple-leaf colours of our national symbol. Proudly displayed by thousands of our people, they turned rows of house fronts into tapestries.

Toward nine o'clock the procession, which had been formed near St. Jacques School, at the corner of St. Catherine and St. Denis Streets, began to file off. The centre of attention among those marching in the procession was some thirty Zouaves, twenty in the uniform of the Pope's army. At their head floated a magnificent papal flag.

The filing-off took place under the direction of the zealous Master of Ceremonies, Monsieur le Chevalier de Bellefeuille, with the help of several assistants, who also contributed much to the perfect organization of the event. Along the whole route of the procession each society was headed by its own particular banner, and the air resounded with the national tunes of the bands. . . .

The allegorical centrepiece, the little St. Jean Baptiste,

was the charming younger child of Alderman David. Among those taking part in the procession was our old hero of 1812, Monsieur Labelle, who never fails to be accorded his place of honour.

The procession moved along St. Catherine, Visitation, St. Marie and Notre Dame Streets, with flags floating and bands playing. A great part of Notre Dame Street was very well decorated. The shops were all decked with flags and a good-sized crowd was on hand to see the procession pass by. . . . It reached Notre Dame Church amidst the stirring tones of the carillon, hurled down from the great height of the tall towers.

The vast basilica was filled as soon as the procession had taken its place within its walls. Chairs had been placed in the great aisle for the officers and members of the St. Jean Baptiste Society, as well as for the Papal Zouaves and others. . . .

The sacred edifice was handsomely decorated. The altar blazed with a thousand flames. From the vaulted roof fell draperies and pennants inscribed with mottoes or nationalist maxims, such as: "Improve the Lot of the People," "Peace and Security."

Rev. Monsieur Boyle, Superior of the Seminary, officiated at the service . . .

The choir under the excellent direction of Rev. Monsieur Barbarin, performed a mass of Rossini's . . .

The sermon was then preached by the Rev. P. Trudeau, O.M.I., whose reputation of an eloquent speaker is well established and who made a deep impression on his listeners by the warmth of his diction, the flash and vivacity of his thoughts and the fine arrangement of his discourse.

The Rev. Monsieur Trudeau spoke as follows: . . .

"I see in the house of God a great and happy crowd. . . .

"My brethren, why are you here? What is this day? What is the meaning of this rich finery, these badges, these flags, this circle of church dignitaries around the sanctuary? This is the day of the National Festival, the day of 'la Patrie'. . . .

"The life of a people, like the life of man, is in the soil. Once abandoned, the soil yields nothing but thorns and brambles. We have to drive the strong iron of the plough into its depths, reaching for its heart. They are beautiful, these vast domains where the riches of agriculture only await the hand of labour to develop them. These unbounded fields, watered and nurtured by the fine waters of a thousand brimming rivers, these mountains crowned by forests eternal! Such beauty is sterile and worthless, if the hand of man does not sow and reap in these lands the elements of life. Your fathers — they understood this; their first care, in laying claim to the soil, was to work it and make it fertile. They were 'habitants.' O you new generations, you are wrong to be ashamed of this name. And why? The fields, they say, are turning into deserts, the sons of the families blush to follow the plough, to be the sons of the habitant. The good earth becomes once more untilled, or is being sold off, expropriated, into the hands of strangers. . . .

"French Canadians, my brother French Canadians, if you do not preserve and fertilize your lands, if you lose the use of them, if you cease to be proprietors, if you have territory no longer, you are no longer a people, you become outcasts, slaves; for the soil — that is the fatherland. The Roman Eagle, and then, the Turkish Crescent have become the masters of Judea and Palestine. Where are the sons of Judea and Levi? They are no longer a nation, they have no longer a fatherland, they are the Wandering Jew. So be it, but what a terrible lesson for us! . . .

"Preserve, defend our nationality by the only means you have, the conservation and culture of your fields. . . ."

After the mass, the procession was formed again, went down St. Sulpice Street and along St. Paul, where there was a grand array of decorations, then moved to Place Viger. Here a number of speeches were delivered. . . .

Mr. C. A. Leblanc next led three cheers for the St. Jean Baptiste Society, for the Papal Zouaves and for the Master of Ceremonies, Monsieur le Chevalier de Belle-feuille. Then after some words from Monsieur J. A. David, the crowd dispersed.

The grand promenade concert that ended the St. Jean Baptiste festivities took place yesterday evening in the magnificent St. Patrick Hall. It was a great success. The audience was numerous and very select. . . . The pro-gramme . . . left nothing to be desired.

Lively airs were played by the Chausseurs-Canadiens, and the choir of the choral society followed with some well-rendered songs, which were warmly applauded. Dancing then began, and was kept up with spirit.

The Montreal police in the nineteenth century suffered from poor pay. In the eighteen-fifties they were paid only fifty cents a day. Guillaume Lamothe, after his appointment as Chief of Police in 1861, demanded higher pay for his men and succeeded in having it raised to a dollar a day. His successor, Frederick W. L. Penton, when appointed in 1865, continued the struggle. In 1873 he was still trying to impress upon the civic authorities that they could scarcely expect to have an adequate force for the pay that was being provided.

Chief Penton was born in Calais, France, in 1826, of an English father and a French mother. He was educated in the Island of Jersey, and after coming to Canada took up farming. In 1862 he was appointed Superintendent of the City Passenger Railway, resigning in 1865 to become Chief of Police. He held the post till 1879.

His appeal for better conditions for his men is an eloquent, forceful document, though with curiosities of spelling and punctuation. It was printed as the *Annual Report of the Chief of Police for the Year 1873* (Montreal, 1874). This excerpt is from pages 3-6.

The Police Force will become thoroughly efficient when the officers and men are renumerated in a way to ensure at all times the services of competent men.

It is hardly possible to expect that really able and strong men can be kept in the Force for the paltry sum of eight dollars a week. Laborers are paid higher wages, and your committee are well aware that sub-constables should be men very different in qualifications from laborers or working men; these latter generally perform one sort of work, and their labor is mere manual labor only, and nobody expects them to be men of sound judgment or of bodily courage. And yet these men are paid from $2 to $2.50 a day; whilst sub-constables who are required to be sober, intelligent and stoutly built; to be ready at all times for duty, in fair or foul weather, day and night, during the extreme summer heat and severe cold of the winter months, in short, to be ever ready to obey like well disciplined soldiers, only receive from the public a poor salary of $8 a week.

No wonder then that men will make no stay in the Force. Circumstances will compel an unfortunate man, to engage into the Force, when he can find nothing else to do, and he uses his admission in the Force as a kind of stepping stone, or rather as a waiting platform until something better shall turn up, and thus is the Police Force a thoroughfare for needy persons who go through it to reach some better locality for the exercise of their ability and strength; and that I may not be accused of wantonly exagerating matters, I may here state that during the year, 53 men left the Force of their own accord and that I had to discharge 42 more for inefficiency, or in other words 95 men out of a Force of 151 left the service. As long as this paltry renumeration is continued, it is impossible for me to select men of the right sort. I am compelled to fill up the gasps [gaps] with the first comers and to replace these with new comers again, before a few months have elapsed, and again applicants are not always forthcoming; in fact, the whole year around I am short of men, for the simple reason that the wages are not considered sufficient to support a family even in the most humble and economical manner.

It has occurred to me that a change for the better might be made, and this state of things mended at least, if not entirely removed, if I were allowed to keep a Reserve force of six men as supernumeraries at $8 a week. The rest of the men receiving an increase of $1 or $9 a week. These supernumeraries would be taught, the various duties of their station, and after a three month's trial, they would either be admitted into the regular ranks, if found qualified, or discharged altogether if inefficient. This I suggested last year, but with no practical result.

Small as this increase may appear, I feel confident that it would enable me to select proper men for the work required from Police sub Constables, and to have under my command an efficient body of men well trained in Police duties. I would also recommend for the officers a cor-responding increase of their pay, and the reason is too sufficiently apparent to need fuller explanation.

It will be seen by the statement of the strength of the Police Force that 19 men only are on the streets during the day, and 50 men at night. Your Committee will easily understand that with such a small force under my control, it is utterly impossible for me to protect the City as I would wish to do. But if the number of men is too limited, their beats on the other hand are too extended . . .

There are localities in this City where a policeman has never been seen, unless it be some special men on sanitary duties.

This will explain the favorite cry of *"where's the Police"*? Whenever any disturbance occurs. The answer is plain, gentlemen: The Police are doing duty on their several and respective beats, but as disturbers of the peace, thieves and rowdy are not in the habit of playing their nefarious avocations when a policeman is in sight, it is impossible for the constables to be at every spot along their beats, and I trust these explanations shall convince the public, that it is impossible to find a policeman every-where, when called for.

When the French writer H. de Lamothe visited Montreal in 1872, he arrived at a time when the turbulence of politics could be seen to best advantage. As soon as he entered Mont-real he heard everyone talking about the "Pacific Scandal" — or the "Pacific Slander," according to their party's viewpoint. He found that "young people and old people seemed to have only one theme for conversation. No matter what group one approached, it was impossible not to hear, three times a minute, the word 'Pacific.' "

The Conservative Government of Sir John A. Macdonald was faced with the revelation that Sir John had been soliciting and receiving large contributions to the party funds from Sir Hugh Allan, the head of the syndicate seeking the franchise to build the Canadian Pacific Railway. The Liberals charged the Conservatives with bribery; the Conservatives called the Liberals slanderers who were trying to manufacture a scandal by distorting the facts.

The whole country was in agitation over the issue, but in Quebec it was being fought out between the Conservatives (the "Bleus") and the Liberals (the "Rouges") with Gallic exuberance, or what H. de Lamothe called "an exaggerated Atticism." Disputes between the "Bleus" and the "Rouges" were carried so far at times that they ended up in the courts. H. de Lamothe was taken one day to the magistrate's court in Montreal to hear a case concerning a distinguished young "Bleu" journalist who had been punched by a "Rouge" Member of Parliament, following an attack in the press.

This is a translation of the extract on pages 87-90 of H. de Lamothe's book *Cinq Mois Chez Les Français d'Amérique* ... (Paris, 1879) .

I was fetched one fine morning to be taken to a session of the police court. The disreputable crowd usually found at such a place — the incorrigible drunkards, the young ladies of easy virtue, and common vagrants — had given place this time to a more distinguished gathering. It was in connection with the Pacific Scandal. The plaintiff was a young journalist, a supporter of the Government — a writer of much ability, whose zeal sometimes carried him away. I had been introduced to him the day before, and now he was bringing into court an Opposition member of the federal Parliament.

This member of the Opposition had thrust his way into the journalist's innner sanctum to demand an explanation of a rather sharp article, wherein his behaviour, his votes and his speeches relating to the *cause célèbre* had been censured in quite unparliamentary terms. The explanations had not seemed at all satisfactory to him, for, then and there, he decided to seek redress for himself by making use of the weapons Nature had provided — his fists. In Paris, they would have taken the Brussels train and drawn their swords. But in Canada, as in England, the duel has gone out of fashion, and our journalist was content to prosecute his aggressor under the legal charge of "assault and battery," as it is known in the criminal code of Lower Canada.

I was promised that the trial would offer very curious examples of the political, legal and literary customs of the country; and really it interested me a great deal, not only by the very colourful local incidents shown in the depositions but by the singularity of an all-English procedure in a case pleaded entirely in French. When I say entirely, I go a bit far. The lawyers were constantly going from one idiom to the other with perfect fluency and ease.

The witnesses, including the plaintiff, were entering, one after the other, a sort of enclosed seat, known in English as the "witness-box," which the French Canadians have literally translated as "boîte à témoins." There they were submitted by the lawyers of both sides to a volley of questions, which were sometimes insidious and often quite indiscreet. One of the most insistent questioners was a gaunt, intelligent-looking young man, with a bilious complexion and a head of hair that would have made Absalom himself jealous. He was none other than a provincial Cabinet minister, renowned for his eloquence, who had come for the express purpose of assisting his friend the journalist, one of the best writers the party had.

At every turn in the course of their examination and pleading the honourable members of the bar called one another "my learned friend," which did not prevent their saying things as disagreeable to one another as if they had been saying "my so-and-so colleague." As for "His Honour" the judge, he spoke French with a heavy French-Canadian accent and seemed quite annoyed and embarrassed at having to render judgment between two such highly placed gentlemen.

My new friend D——, questioned under oath, had disavowed the authorship of the most violent articles; he had only accepted the responsibility for them in the absence of the true authors. However, he had told me the day before that, in his eyes, and in the eyes of many of his colleagues in Canadian journalism, the foremost of the French authors of the time was the fiery writer of *Odeurs de Paris*. I noticed by the tone of the articles read to the court that a study — a study far too conscientious, alas! — of the works and methods of that master had given to the polemics of his disciples a very biting acrimony which went a long way to explain the rage of the Opposition Member and its regrettable consequences. The Montreal press, quite as much as that of Quebec, is guilty of an exaggerated Atticism, and if blows with the fists sometimes answer blows with the pen, it is because the latter are all too often given as if they were blows with the fists.

After the lawyers, pleading with a stubbornness worthy of their Norman colleagues and cousins, had sufficiently confused the issue, the accused, his massive bulk contrasting with the unimposing appearance of his opponent, delivered a speech in his own defence. In a stentorian voice, he inveighed against the corruption of the ministerial party. The Cabinet minister — the lawyer with the long hair — dealt contemptuously with this heatedly worked-up appeal — good enough, perhaps, as a speech to the electors in the country of Deux-Montagnes, but quite out of place in a court of justice.

The pleadings being over, "His Honour" stammered the verdict that sentenced Monsieur W. P . . . , Member of Parliament, to pay a fine of twenty dollars and costs. The friends of the plaintiff began declaring that such a penalty amounted to nothing; those of the accused seethed with indignation, but for quite the opposite reason. In short, both parties, equally dissatisfied, left the courtroom fretting and fuming alike against judge and judgment. Unfortunate magistrate! I heard plenty against him, and I imagine that his ears must really have tingled all during the proverbial twenty-four hours.

There are dramatic flourishes in the way William Alexander Foster writes of his experience in shooting the Lachine Rapids on a timber raft about 1874. At that time timber cut in the region near the Great Lakes and on the Ottawa was floated down to Quebec for shipbuilding or export. A raft was made up of a number of units, called drams, chained or roped together, each of which measured about 60 feet wide and from 200 to 250 feet long. A shanty of pine boards was built on each raft to give some shelter to the crew and their barrels of pork, biscuit and bread. Each raft took about a month to build. It had to be careful work, for, as Foster said, a "raft is quite safe so long as its constituent logs keep together."

Timber rafts came down all the rapids of the St. Lawrence, but the greatest danger was at Lachine, where the channel was so boisterous and intricate that Indian steersmen were brought aboard from Caughnawaga, as they were also brought aboard the steamboats.

William Alexander Foster was a Toronto barrister who became one of the founders and chief leaders of the "Canada First" movement of 1868-75 — a movement that believed strong national feeling would be the surest means of counteracting Canada's "disintegrating tendencies." He died in Toronto, still in his forties, in 1888.

Foster's account first appeared in print in his anonymous article, "Down the St. Lawrence on a Raft," in *The Canadian Monthly and National Review*, October, 1874. It was reprinted in his collected writings, *Canada First: A Memorial to the late William A. Foster, Q.C.* (Toronto, 1890), where this selection will be found on pages 191-92, 195-98.

The last rapid was to be run on the morrow, and, the night being before us, a little relaxation was indulged in. Visitors from the shore came aboard in canoes, and we were soon on speaking terms with the civilized descendants of the Caughnawaga Indians. Theirs was not a visit of ceremony; they meant business. The Lachine could not be run without their assistance. The foreman of the raft gave audience to the most Indian-looking of the visitors, and after a brief pow-wow, we learned that a selection of pilots and oarsmen had been made. . . . In a very short time, therefore, everything is arranged, and the Indians depart as silently as they came, with strict orders to be on board at three o'clock next morning. The raftsmen huddle together in the shanties, the fires are stirred up, and cards, dancing, jokes, stories, and songs find their place in the programme of the night. The tourists are told that the most dangerous rapid, the Lachine, has yet to be run, and are plied with tales of hair-breadth escapes from drowning; of drams that had broken from their mooring at night in a gale, and had shot the rapids without pilotage; of drams that had struck rocks in such a manner as to cause the sticks of timber to bounce up high in the air; of drams that had been sucked into eddies and had bathed their crews in six or seven feet of water; of drams that had gone to pieces, and whose unleashed logs had jammed and pounded every one on board into unrecognizable pulp — in fact all the rafting horrors of years are renewed for the especial benefit of the laymen whose fortune it is to be present at the night's recital. But no terror was equal to the ridicule which would have been ours had we gone ashore on the eve of the event which was to cap the climax of the voyage; or to the contempt which would have rendered our names immortally luminous in raftsman's story had we yielded to the promptings of an un-biassed discretion; so, looking as cheerful as possible, we stowed away a more than liberal allowance of hard-tack, potatoes and tea, and contributed a fair share of the heroic to the night's entertainment. Martyrs to rashness, we could not help endeavouring to recall the particulars of our life policies, so spent a moment or two in wondering whether the suicide clause applied to rapids. . . .

At three in the morning the Indians came on board, according to orders, and by six everything had been got ready, and the drams cleared for the run. Twenty-six men rowed on each. The sun was shining out gloriously; not a breath of wind stirred the surface of the river. The oars swung in their holders with a uniform thud. The men pulled, of course, standing up, and as they were on the lowest tier or bottom of the dram, they moved constantly in five or six inches of water. However, damp feet are not a cause of anxiety to a raftsman. Between Lachine and Caughnawaga the breadth of the St. Lawrence narrows to about half a mile. As we pass the churches on either shore, the men drop on their knees and say their prayers — some for a moment or two, others for a longer time. There is little or no noise save the splash of oars, and there is much less profanity than is usually heard. "Don't

swear till we get through the Lachine," says one rebuk-
ingly to an irate companion. The roar of the rapid is now
heard. The pace is getting fast and faster every instant.
The drams stretch out in line of battle, and the pilot's
voice is more frequently heard shouting his orders: "En
haut," meaning row away at the bow; "à derrière," at the
stern. Now, the bow oars are alone at work; now, the men
at the stern make their oars bend with a will; now all, at
bow, stern and sides, pull with their utmost strength.
Everything depends on how and where we enter the
rapids, and as the pilot mops his brow with his red handkerchief, we know that the time has come for all his
presence of mind, all his skill. A few feet to the wrong
side may suffice to cause him the loss of his pay, and ourselves the loss of our lives. From Caughnawaga to the
lower extremity of the rapid, a distance of nearly four
miles, there is a gradual shelving descent of the rocky bed
of the river. The stream in passing down acquires an
irresistible impetus, and towards the lower part runs with
a velocity of eighteen miles an hour, until it is separated
by some islands below into several channels. Into this
ravine we glide with tremendous rapidity, and take the
first pitch like a cork, all hands seeking a dry spot in the
middle of the dram, until a heavy wave strikes and passes
over. Straight onward the dram speeds, the men giving
their whole strength to their oars to keep it in the proper
course. Now a corner is to be turned, and the violence of
the waters is such that the men in the bow can with difficulty retain their places. There is a very Babel of voices.
The pilot, notwithstanding his Indian blood, springs to
and fro on the timber, and shouts excitedly to the men in
a mixture of Indian and French, and the sturdy fellows

yell encouragement to each other, with savage appreciation of the danger. Wave after wave gathers itself in a
mass and tumbles on us as if seeking to conquer by sheer
weight of water; wave after wave dashes itself to fragments
against our sturdy side. The shanty leaps into the air;
over goes the stove; down come the stove-pipes; the withes
can almost be heard to shriek with the agony of extreme
tension, and the sticks of timber move restlessly in their
faithful clutch. The excitement culminates in a roar of
triumph, as the drams swing round the point of danger
and cleave the waves with a hissing sound which tells how
fearful is the speed. The men again leap to their oars. In
a moment or two we have passed through a stretch of
comparative calm; shot over a rocky ledge on the crests of
billows so much engaged in smashing each other as to be
careless of the use to which they were put by us; and gone
headlong down the third pitch. The dram emerges splut-
tering, and shakes its high sides like a Newfoundland dog.
The men are again at their posts, dripping but joyful, and
the pilot stands quietly mopping huge patches of perspira-
tion from his face. "A pretty rough passage, pilot," one
ventures to observe. "The best I have had, Sir; you
brought luck with you." The Victoria Bridge was now in
sight, and after passing underneath one of its spans, we
were, about two o'clock, brought to anchor near Montreal.

The sleigh-drives of the garrison officers were a tradition
in nineteenth-century Montreal. The officers of the imperial
garrison kept fine horses and took pride in their sleighs and
"turn-outs." Their winter processions, about 1840, were so
long that when the president of the driving club was leading
the way round Place d'Armes, the vice-president, bringing up
the rear, would be at Nelson's Moument, four or five blocks
away.

In 1862 William Howard Russell, the correspondent of *The Times*, had seen the garrison driving club setting out: "a certain looming up of dark forms through the drift gliding along to the music of the bells, which followed one after the other, and were lost in the hazy yet glittering clouds tossed up by the horses' hoofs from the snow." And when Lieutenant-Colonel Garnet Wolseley (later Field Marshal Sir Garnet Wolseley) was in the Montreal garrison in the eighteen-sixties he took part in many sleigh-drives into the country: "Altogether, it was an elysium of bliss for young officers, the only trouble being to keep single."

After the imperial garrison was withdrawn from Montreal in 1870, the officers of the militia regiments kept up the tradition of the driving clubs. A typical drive was that of the officers of the Prince of Wales Rifles, under the command of Lieutenant-Colonel Frank Bond, on the last Saturday before the New Year's Day of 1876. Lieutenant-Colonel Bond was the sort of officer to whom the name "dashing" was usually applied. Three years later he was to shoot the Lachine Rapids in a thirty-foot boat with Big John of Caughnawaga. Long interested in military life, he had seen active service on the border against the invading Fenians.

His militia interests were a sort of recreation from his life in finance. He had had his financial training with the Bank of Montreal, then served as secretary of the Montreal Stock Exchange, and finally became a stockbroker himself. He had much of the imposing height and size and the booming voice of his father, Canon W. B. Bond of St. George's Church (later the Anglican Bishop of Montreal).

This report appeared in *The Canadian Illustrated News*, January 1, 1876. (The "clouds" described were the light woollen scarves worn by Victorian women to protect their faces from the cold, especially during sleigh-drives.)

On Saturday week last, Colonel Bond and the Officers of this Regiment gave a most delightful entertainment to their numerous friends, in the shape of "a drive" to Longue Pointe, followed by a dance and a supper. The day was all that could be desired, though perhaps a trifle cold, but that only afforded an excuse for the display of all those becoming furs and "clouds" of endless variety and colour, in which our fair Canadian lady-friends take such delight in disguising themselves to the mystification of their bewildered admirers. There were blue clouds, rosy clouds, black clouds and even green clouds, until nature herself took offence at such rivalry; and by way of showing her displeasure, banished every one of her clouds, and allowed the sun to shew his round, good-natured face without let or hindrance, in the midst of an expanse whose azure depths reminded one of skies of Italy and the Mediterranean shore. The roads, too, were in perfect order for sleighing; snowy but firm. At 3 p.m., the hour named, a goodly company, numbering over a hundred, conveyed in from 50 to 60 sleighs of every possible description and shape, from the handsome "drag" with its pair of high-stepping steeds, to the more humble one-horse "cariole," began to assemble in Dominion Square. Each sleigh, as it arrived, took up an assigned position and when all had "mustered," the photograph, of which our engraving in this issue, is a faithful copy, was taken, the scene itself, at the moment, being exceedingly interesting and picturesque. The photographers being satisfied, the order to advance was given and, headed by Colonel Bond, the cavalcade set forth at a brisk pace to the merry music of the bells.

"To the rhyming and the chiming
Of the Bells, Bells, Bells."

Up into Sherbrooke street, down Union Avenue and Beaver Hall, along St. James's street and out into the country swept the gay cortège, to the manifest admiration and delight of pedestrians. Colonel Bond, in his character of leader, permitted no lagging, but kept up the speed throughout the whole distance, which was accomplished in a marvellously short time. After a most exhilarating drive of 6 miles, which must have effectually dispelled any lurking spirit of melancholy, if such there were, lingering amongst the company, Hochelaga was reached and passed, and Longue Pointe, with the Hotel hoisting its flag of welcome and decorated with wreaths of evergreens and coloured lanterns came in sight. There was a regimental guard in attendance, and the whole of the arrangements for the comfort and pleasure of the guests were carried out with that military precision and completeness so characteristic of the Regiment, and which it is impossible to estimate too highly. If the tactics of the Officers of the Prince of Wales Rifles are as cleverly planned, and as satisfactorily executed in warlike as in peaceful pursuits, we need have no fear, we are sure, in confiding ourselves and our country to their keeping.

Mais revenons à nos moutons. In less time than it takes to describe, horses and sleighs were given up to the care of the grooms in waiting — clouds and wraps disappeared as if by magic and out of the chrysalis forms hitherto visible, emerged a formidable phalanx of veritable butterflies. The gentlemen, on their part, had been no less expeditious, and all speedily found their way to a large room which had been prepared as a ball room, and most tastefully decorated with wreaths, flags and trophies of arms, the Prince of Wales Plume being conspicuous among the devices. Here, Colonel and Mrs. Bond were waiting to receive and welcome the guests. An excellent band, under the able guidance of Herr Gruenwald, struck up an inspiring measure, and for two hours the dance was kept up with untiring zeal. The view from the gallery, provided for the chaperons and non-dancers, was an exceedingly pretty one, made up, as it was, of bright looks and flashing eyes, tasteful toilettes and brilliant uniforms; one and all seeming bent upon enjoying the evening to the full. There was an excellent *buffet* adjoining the ball-room where the most delicious ice-creams and the coolest and most refreshing of lemonades, brewed from a celebrated regimental receipt, might be obtained. At 7.30., supper was announced and all trooped into the spacious dining room with appetites sharpened by the frosty drive and the subsequent homage paid to Terpsichore, and did ample justice to the good things provided by the kind forethought of the committee. After supper, dancing was resumed with increased vigour and continued without flagging till between 9 and 10 o'clock, when a general move was made. Sleighs were again brought into requisition, "clouds" once more appeared on the social horizon, spitefully hiding the fair, glowing faces which had enchanted us but a few minutes before; and with many tender and prolonged adieus, the happy evening at Longue Pointe was reluctantly brought to a close. Not the least enjoyable part of the programme was the scamper home through the clear frosty night. Unfortunately there was no moon visible, but the stars which thickly studded the heavens, did their best to supply her absence; and, as they twinkled like crystal drops, seemed, as it were, to keep time with the tinkling of the sleigh-bells.

The day in 1875 when Samuel Butler happened to visit the museum of the Montreal Natural History Society gave birth to one of the most famous satirical poems in the English language — "A Psalm of Montreal," with "O God! O Montreal!" as its refrain.

The inspiration of the poem was provided, though quite unconsciously, by S. W. Passmore, a Cornishman who was the taxidermist to the society. On that day Passmore was at work in a back room, stuffing an owl. When Butler looked into the room his eye fell upon a discarded plaster cast of the Greek statue of the discus-thrower — the Discobolus. Passmore explained that it could not be placed on exhibition because it was "rather vulgar."

Passmore, "the man of skins," was not speaking for himself alone, when he approved the banishment of the Discobolus. Others in the Montreal Natural History Society were convinced that art was an inferior and even a suspect study. The proper study of mankind was not man and the works of man, but God and the works of God. In 1881 the Montreal Natural History Society dispossessed itself of the Discobolus, by donating it to the gallery of the Art Association of Montreal, then in Phillips Square. Rupert Brooke made a point of looking it up on his visit to Montreal in 1913. "I made my investigations in Montreal," he wrote in his *Letters from America*. "I have to report that the Discobolus is very well, and, nowadays, looks the whole world in the face, almost quite unabashed."

Samuel Butler, whose *Erewhon* and *The Fair Haven* had already been published, had come to Montreal from London in 1874 in a forlorn attempt to revive the Canada Tanning Extract Company — a company in which he had been induced to sink a substantial sum of money. When the attempt failed, he returned to London, with many anecdotes about the cultural unawareness of Montrealers.

"A man, a true Montrealer," he wrote in his notebook, "told me he had a yearning to get away from civilization; I said we were all of us given to discontent, and seldom knew *when we had got* what we wanted. He did not see it, and I did not mean that he should, but I felt better for having said it."

A copy of "A Psalm of Montreal" was seen by Matthew Arnold. He sent it to the editor of *The Spectator*, where it appeared on May 18, 1878. It was not long in reaching Montreal, for it was reprinted on June 1, 1878, in *The*

Canadian Spectator, a weekly edited by the Reverend Alfred J. Bray, minister of Zion Congregational Church. A poem in reply followed in the next issue. The indignant Natural History Society defended Passmore for his wisdom in preferring God's nature to man's art, and attacked Butler as the benighted one — the "Heathen Londonee."

"A Psalm of Montreal" has been reproduced here as it appeared in *The Spectator*, though Butler's amplified description of how his poem came to be written is reproduced from *The Note-Books of Samuel Butler*, edited by Henry Festing Jones (London, A. C. Fifield, 1915), page 388.

The City of Montreal is one of the most rising and, in many respects, most agreeable on the American continent, but its inhabitants are as yet too busy with commerce to care greatly about the masterpieces of old Greek Art. In the Montreal Museum of Natural History I came upon two plaster casts, one of the Antinous and the other of the Discobolus — not the good one, but in my poem, of course, I intend the good one — banished from public view to a room where were all manner of skins, plants, snakes, insects, etc., and, in the middle of these, an old man stuffing an owl.

"Ah," said I, "so you have some antiques here; why don't you put them where people can see them?"

"Well, sir," answered the custodian, "you see they are rather vulgar."

He then talked a great deal and said his brother did all Mr. Spurgeon's printing. [Butler, in his poem, makes the brother a brother-in-law, and makes him the haberdasher, rather than the printer, to the London preacher, Spurgeon.]

The dialogue — perhaps true, perhaps imaginary, perhaps a little of the one and a little of the other — between

the writer and this old man gave rise to the lines that
follow:

Stowed away in a Montreal lumber room
The Discobolus standeth and turneth his face to the wall;
Dusty, cobweb-covered, maimed and set at naught,
Beauty crieth in an attic and no man regardeth:
O God! O Montreal!

Beautiful by night and day, beautiful in summer and
    winter,
Whole or maimed, always and alike beautiful —
He preacheth gospel of grace to the skin of owls
And to one who seasoneth the skins of Canadian owls:
O God! O Montreal!

When I saw him I was wroth and I said, "O Discobolus!
Beautiful Discobolus, a Prince both among gods and men!
What doest thou here, how camest thou hither, Discob-
    olus,
Preaching gospel in vain to the skins of owls?"
O God! O Montreal!

And I turned to the man of skins and said unto him, "O
    thou man of skins,
Wherefore hast thou done thus to shame the beauty of the
    Discobolus?"
But the Lord had hardened the heart of the man of skins
And he answered, "My brother-in-law is haberdasher to
    Mr. Spurgeon."
O God! O Montreal!

"The Discobolus is put here because he is vulgar —
He has neither vest nor pants with which to cover his
    limbs;
I, Sir, am a person of most respectable connections —
My brother-in-law is haberdasher to Mr. Spurgeon."
O God! O Montreal!

Then I said, "O brother-in-law to Mr. Spurgeon's haber-
dasher,
Who seasonest also the skins of Canadian owls,
Thou callest trousers 'pants,' whereas I call them 'trousers,'
Therefore thou art in hell-fire and may the Lord pity
thee!"

                          O God! O Montreal!

"Preferrest thou the gospel of Montreal to the gospel of
Hellas,
The gospel of thy connection with Mr. Spurgeon's haber-
dasher to the gospel of the Discobolus?"
Yet none the less blasphemed he beauty saying, "The Dis-
cobolus hath no gospel,
But my brother-in-law is haberdasher to Mr. Spurgeon."

                          O God! O Montreal!

The anonymous reply to *A Psalm of Montreal*, as published in The Canadian Spectator, has two footnotes. One,
after the word "Athené" in the fifth verse says: "This
allusion accounts for the frequent mention of the owl in
the effusion of the Londoner." The second footnote follows the words "naked Discobolus of plaster" in the sixth
verse: "This explains the reference to 'pants' and 'trousers'
in the 'Psalm'; and also, perhaps, that to 'Mr. Spurgeon's
haberdasher,' who is no doubt in cockney eyes the em-
bodiment of all that is sublime in clothing."

The following note, in square brackets, appears at the
beginning of *A Lay of a Londoner*.

[The Natural History Society of Montreal was not
aware that it had been honoured with the visit of the
Primitive Philistine, whose "Psalm" appears in the London *Spectator*, and which we have reprinted. It would
have been interesting to have secured some memorials of

his visit for an ethnological collection. That so unique a
specimen of the Heathen Londonee may not be lost on
science, he is entreated to send his photograph, attired in
the costume of his tribe. In the meantime the sciences of
an adequate doggerelist have been secured to give a more
correct version of the incidents referred to in the "psalm."]

An old man sat in a Montreal sanctum,
Around him things rare of many lands,
Patiently shaping the bird of wisdom,
Meditating its plumage and posture,
                                        O, wise old man!

There stood by him also a figure of plasters,
Discobolus, of old heathenish Greeks,
Waiting till fit place be found for it,
In Fine Art Gallery of Montreal,
                                        O, relic misplaced!

Entered to old man a heathen of London,
Glaring around with savage eye,
Blindly unconscious of beauty of nature,
But seeing only plaster Discobolus,
                                        O, Heathen Londonee!

Then cried he, "O! man of skins,
That figure of plaster is by me adored,
Why dishonourest thou the gospel,
Giving it to moles and bats,
                                And seasoning skins of owls?"

Then answered the pitying old man:
"Adore not gods of plaster, O! stranger,
The maker of thy god worshipped bird of Athené,
Else had he not made Discobolus,
                                O! Owl of Minerva!"

Also know that birds are clothed with beauty
More than thy naked Discobolus of plaster,
Owls, as humming-birds and birds of Paradise,
But thy soul is pagan and blinded,
                    O! ignorant Londonee!"

But the heart of the cockney was hardened,
And he cursed the old man by his gods,
Saying, "May Discobolus fell thee, old man,
And prevent thee of seasoning owls,
                    O! stuffer of skins!"

Then arose the old man in anger,
And cursed the Londoner with a great curse,
Saying, "Mayest thou never see leaf or flower
Or bird of beauty, or hear its voice,
                    O! benighted Londonee!

"But only bricks and mortar shalt thou see,
And shalt swallow dust and plaster,
Until a human soul be given to thee,
And thou knowest the work of God from work of man,
                    O! blinded Londonee!"

8

The French and English Cities

The theme of Montreal's "two solitudes," which was to be
dealt with realistically by C. H. Farnham in his article in
Harper's New Monthly Magazine in 1889, was dealt with
more gently, more prudently — perhaps, in a way, more
tolerantly — in the book *Picturesque Canada*, published in
1882, edited by Dr. George Monro Grant, the principal of
Queen's University, Kingston. This article was written in
collaboration by Rev. A. J. Bray, minister of Zion
Congregational Church and the editor of *The Canadian
Spectator*, and Jean Talon Lespérance, the French-Canadian
littérateur and journalist, who was at different times the editor
of *The Canadian Illustrated News* and *The Dominion
Illustrated News*.

These two writers described Montreal's two cities — the
English and the French — and how they were visibly cut apart,
as if with a knife. Even where the two were side by side, as in
the downtown area above the waterfront, they somehow
seemed to stand apart.

The writers of this article did not see in this separation an
urgent problem or a coming clash. They interpreted it,
rather, as the settling down of peoples who cherished their
differences, with little inclination to merge. They were
dwelling apart by mutual choice, rather than through mutual

grievance. The choice had its origins in traditions and aims so different that they could not hope or wish to meet, except where the differences could be maintained.

The English portion of the city is pictured as committed to commerce and valuing modernity, progress, and large, imposing edifices. The French portion is shown deeply set in an older mood, preferring plainer and less ostentatious ways, and preserving in many of its families "an Old World refinement" very different from "the loud manners of the *nouveaux riches*."

This description nowhere suggests that a revolution might come, or that either solitude felt itself the victim of the other. The theme, rather, is that of peaceful co-existence, with neither solitude envying the other, but favouring its own way, and looking upon the other as alien and almost impenetrable. It is a vigorous, vivid description, based on the conviction that the separation was acceptable, and permanent. Hence the fascination of a city where such deep, unchanging and unchangeable contrasts were possible.

This description of Montreal's "two solitudes" is to be found in volume one of *Picturesque Canada* (Toronto, 1882), pages 106-9, 112-14.

Montreal abounds with striking contrasts. The city is comparatively small — less than one hundred and fifty thousand inhabitants — as what was called "the census" has declared. It has had only one or two hundred years of history; and yet everything is here — the antique and the modern — while hostile oddities lie cheek-by-jowl on every hand. Here are frame houses, some of them scarcely better than an Irishman's hovel on his native bog, and ignorance and squalour and dirt; close at hand are great streets of great houses, all of fine-cut stone. Here are thousands of French who cannot speak one word of English, and thousands of English who cannot speak one word of French. Unthrift and thrift come along the same thoroughfares. Some are content with a bare existence and some are not content with colossal fortunes. In social life we have the old French families with their Old World refinement pressed upon and almost pushed out of existence by the loud manners of the *nouveaux riches*. The older houses have their heirlooms of gold trinkets and silver plate; the new houses have their art galleries of elaborate picture-frames, the meanest of which would honour Cellini, and gladden the eyes and heart of a solid Manchester man.

We have the same striking contrasts in the appearance of the people on the streets. Here are unmistakable descendants of the ancient Iroquois Indians; at a turn we come upon a company who, by their dress and talk, take us back to the peasant classes of older France; while crowding everywhere are ladies and gentlemen of the most approved modern type, according to the fashions of London, Paris, and New York. The business of the place shows the same quaint differences. At one market we are in an exclusively agricultural district; there is nothing to suggest a ship, a warehouse, or a factory; buyers and sellers are country people with country ways, except that now and then a lady from the more aristocratic parts ventures to go a-marketing in the interests of economy. . . . All the streets round the Bonsecours Market are crowded with carts filled with country produce, and the overflow finds its way into Jacques Cartier Square. The horses feeding peacefully as they would beside a country hostelry, primitive carts and harness, the *habitant* piously committing his horse or his basket to the care of God while he slips into the old church to say a prayer, are not the pictures one expects to find in a great city in the restless New World. A very little way to the west, you are in a different latitude. Signs of commerce and modern taste and industrial life abound. Here is a corner where we look into Victoria Square. The crowded streets, the magnificent cut-stone shops, hotels and warehouses, the well-appointed hall and rooms of the Young Men's Christian Association — the oldest Association of the kind in America, — the beautiful Kirk, Salisbury Cathedral in miniature, the bronze statue of the Queen by Marshall Wood, all reflect the nineteenth century. What surprises the visitor is the sharp distinction so long maintained. The new does not shoulder the ancient out of the way — does not even modify it. They move along parallel lines, neither affecting the other. There is no fusion of races in commercial, social or political life; the differences are sharply defined, and appear to be permanent. It must be confessed that this adds to the interest of the city, and enables the curious to study human life and work under a variety of aspects. . . .

It is easy to trace the two main divisions of the population of Montreal. Taking St. Lawrence Main Street as a dividing line, all that is east of it is French, and all that is west of it is English-speaking. The two nationalities scarcely overlap this conventional barrier, except in a few isolated cases. And other external characteristics of the French population are as distinct as their language. The houses are less pretentious, though quite comfortable, and there is a general absence of ornament or of surrounding plantations. The extreme eastern portion is designated the Quebec suburbs, and there the native people can be studied as easily as in the rural villages, from which the majority hail. They are an honest, hard-working race, very gay and courteous, and of primitive simplicity of life. Their thrift is remarkable, and they manage to subsist on one half of what would hardly satisfy the needs of people of other nationalities. The old folks speak little or no English, but it is different with the rising generation. These use the two languages indifferently, and herein possess a marked advantage over the English, Scotch and Irish. Within late years also, they have learned to husband their resources. They have in their midst a flourishing branch of the City and District Savings Bank, a number of building societies and two or three benevolent guilds. Their poor are cared for by the St. Vincent de Paul Association, which has several ramifications, and the Union St. Joseph is devoted to the relief of artisans during life, and of their families after death.

There is a great deal of hoarded wealth among the French inhabitants, but as a rule they do not invest it freely. They have among them some of the richest men in the city who, however, are modest in their wants, and make no display either in the way of sumptuous mansions or gaudy equipages. Although extremely hospitable and fond of society, they are not in the habit of giving balls or fancy entertainments, their evenings being spent mostly in mutual visits, where a quiet game of cards predominates. As in Paris so in Montreal, it is not easy to obtain access into the inner French circles; but once initiated, the stranger is agreeably surprised at the amount of grace and culture which he meets. It is a current mistake that higher education is uncommon among these people. The gift of conversation is almost universal; the best topics of art and literature are freely discussed, and ladies are familiar with political questions.

The western part of the city is English. By this term is meant all those whose vernacular is our mother-tongue.

Numerically, the English portion is not so great as the Scotch, who unquestionably take the lead in commerce, finance and public enterprise generally. In perhaps no section of the Colonies have Englishmen and Scotchmen made more of their opportunities than in Montreal. There is an air of prosperity about all their surroundings which at once impresses the visitor. Taken all in all, there is perhaps no wealthier city area in the world than that comprised between Beaver Hall Hill and the foot of Mount Royal, and between the parallel lines of Dorchester and Sherbrooke Streets in the West End. Sherbrooke Street is scarcely surpassed by the Fifth Avenue of New York in the magnificence of its buildings. The grounds include demesne and park, the charms of the country and the rush and roar of a great commercial centre. In winter the equipages present a most attractive spectacle. It has been said that in this respect only St. Petersburg can claim precedence over Montreal. A favourite drive on a Saturday afternoon in winter is from Victoria Square to Nelson's Column and back, the sumptuous sleighs of every description, drawn by high-steppers, and bearing lovely women ensconced in the richest furs of the Canadian forest, following each other in endless succession. There is also a winter driving club, which periodically starts from the iron gates of McGill College and glides like the wind along the country roads to a hospitable rendezvous at Sault aux Récollet, Lachine or Longue Pointe, where a bounteous repast and a "hop" are provided. The return home under the moon and stars is the most enjoyable feature of the entertainment, and many a journey through life has been initiated by these exhilarating drives.

The extreme south-western portion of the city is occupied almost exclusively by the Irish population. It is called Griffintown, from a man of that name who first settled there and leased a large tract of ground from the Grey Nuns for ninety-nine years. Over sixty years of this lease have already expired, so that in about twenty-five or thirty years the ground rent of this immense section will revert to the nuns. Griffintown comprises a little world within itself — shops, factories, schools, academies, churches and asylums. The Irish population of Montreal take a high stand in business, politics and society. They number in their ranks many successful merchants and large capitalists, and have leading representatives in all the learned professions.

Till a massive revetment was built in 1888, Montreal was exposed to the floods every spring. The previous embankment served its purpose so long as the drifting ice cleared out of the river quickly. But if there was a serious ice-jam, it acted as a dam. The rising water was soon over the wall and into the city.

The flood of April, 1885 was the greatest in twelve years. No trains could leave for New York; a hackman was drowned on Centre Street; so many boats and rafts were being used that they were colliding at the street-corners; and people in the flooded area had loaves of bread tossed to them through upper windows.

The account of the floods of 1885 and 1886 given in the autobiography of Richard Hemsley shows what the floods meant in the life of a merchant. Hemsley was an Englishman from Gloucester who had opened his shop as jeweller and watch-maker on St. Joseph Street (as Notre Dame Street West was then known). Inexperienced in floods, he was caught unawares in 1885. He rowed to his shop, only to see his counters toppling with the rising water. In 1886 he was not only on the alert, but had devised ingenious precautions.

Richard Hemsley's autobiography *Looking Back* was privately printed in Montreal in 1930. The floods are described on pages 88-93.

By hard work and strict economy I had managed to save ten thousand dollars in stock and fixtures which I was doomed to lose, and found myself in debt three thousand dollars on account of a flood. I left the store at nine o'clock one night without a suspicion of trouble, and next morning I could not get nearer my door than several hundreds of yards on account of the flood.

All traffic west of Dupre Lane was suspended, there being about five feet of water in the street. With the aid of a boat I reached the store, the door of which was protected by an iron gate secured by two strong padlocks, one of which was too low in the water to unlock. On looking into my store from the boat I saw a ship's chronometer slip off the counter into the water and the next moment the whole length of counters, with glass cases, toppled over. The rising water had lifted them, and as they were heavier on top, the centre of gravity was changed. I then knew that counters are not fastened to the floor.

As we failed to unlock the gate, it was realized that the dial lock of the safe was too much under water to open, so it was decided to leave everything until the waters receded. Eight days passed before we could enter the store. The shop fixtures were totally destroyed, also $10,000 worth of watches rendered useless, except for the metal in the cases.

Although the savings of fifteen years' hard work were lost, I could not reproach myself. I was protected against burglary, and insured against fire, but there was no insurance against flood. We quickly cleaned up the damaged goods and sold them by auction, and I set my staff to repairing watches and making jewellery to order. Although my entire assets disappeared, I was able to effect a loan from Robert Campbell, retired wholesale druggist. With this money I went to England and ordered a London-made show window, embodying an invention of my own. This improvement allowed the window to be opened as often as desired in the coldest weather, and to be entirely free from frost, and clear of dust and flies in summer. This investment proved a great success, and in order to be prepared for future floods I kept on hand enough wood to make platforms on which fixtures and stock could be placed above high-water mark.

I continued to live in Hochelaga and the next spring kept a sharp lookout on the river ice. Early one morning I saw the grandest sight of my life. The ice jam had caused the river to rise fully thirty feet or more, which resulted in the entire ice-field, two miles in width, moving rapidly down stream with blocks of ice six to ten feet in thickness, fifty feet more or less in length and width, tumbling over each other in the wildest confusion, and rising to a height of nearly one hundred and fifty feet. This was doubtless caused by the moving ice being brought into contact with the partly submerged Isle Ronde.

For some minutes I thought of nothing but the magnificent sight in front of me. I quickly came to my senses when I thought about the store with its new fixtures, London show-window, and the $25,000 stock. I hurriedly dressed and started for the city by horse car. At the first switch — the track being single — I saw a man rescue his wife and child from an upstair window of a house built too low on the river bank. This showed me how quickly the water was rising. On arriving at the store, I sent cabmen to the homes of my employees, and by seven o'clock we were all hard at work building platforms, using the wood I had prepared a year before. About ten o'clock, Mr. Moore, my next door neighbor, a hardware merchant, came into the store and asked me if I were crazy, stating there was no fear of a flood. I went with him into his shop to see the cellar, which he said was quite dry. As he spoke he lifted a trapdoor and in order to prove his assertion, jumped down, with the result that he was up to his waist in water. The floating straw and packing material had completely hidden the water. The flood first came into the cellars through the sewers.

In six hours' time we had everything secured above high-water mark, including the counters, show cases, contents of the safe, and the London show-window stripped of everything moveable. At one o'clock we locked up the iron gate, there being one inch of water on the floor, and seven days passed before we entered the store again. The loss in this second flood was negligible. During the first flood, all sidewalks, being of wood, floated away. This time we secured the one in front of the store by nailing a stout rope to the frame of the shop, and then to the sidewalk, with sufficient slack to allow it to rise and fall with the water. As all valuables were out of the safe, an armed watchman was engaged night and day to promenade the floating sidewalk to protect the store. This man was one of the Holmes Electric Company, now the Dominion Electric Protection Company.

During these two floods I amused myself by rowing about the streets, and also undertook a common method of navigation, that is, using a length of sidewalk propelled by a pole. On one occasion I was in great danger using this primitive raft in front of the old Custom House. The water suddenly dropped, making a strong current towards the river. I then found my pole too short and my strength too weak to stem the current. Luckily a man in a skiff took me on board in the nick of time, otherwise in a few minutes I should have been carried out among the moving ice. Sad sights could be seen in the flooded districts, such as funerals on boats. The people had to be fed by food handed from boats through their upstair windows.

We had an experience of Venice without the expense of crossing the Atlantic; although there was no Bridge of Sighs in Montreal, yet hundreds of people were daily sighing for the time to come when they could reach their homes and places of business on dry land.

My experience was one of a thousand, and the city authorities realized that something should be done. The result was the present revetment wall, which extends from Bonsecours Market to the west side of Verdun. The building of this great wall, with its pumping stations, must rank as the most important undertaking ever attempted by our city, especially when we consider the immense area of land made safe for building purposes.

Although I lived many years on the banks of the river, this was the only time I have seen a real ice shove. The flood waters of the St. Lawrence and the River Richelieu nearly met each other.

Tobogganing was the most exciting sport in nineteenth-century Montreal. Nothing could equal it in speed, as skiing was unknown till the century's last few years, and even then it was experimental and rare. To shoot down Montreal's steep hills by toboggan was to ride with the whirlwind. Spectators speak of the toboggans "flashing by," almost too swift for the eye to see. Nor was it all smooth going. A *cahot* or ground-swell, or a snowed-over fence, could send a toboggan leaping into the air, to land with a thud that rattled the bones.

The sport flourished all the more because the city was small and good tobogganing hills were easy to reach. McTavish and Côte des Neiges hills served very well. Even when the expanding city drove tobogganers farther afield, they still had good hills, such as Brehaut's, in Côte St. Antoine. (Today Côte St. Antoine is Westmount, and Brehaut's Hill is Mountain Avenue.)

This narrative is by the leading writer on Canadian sport in the Victorian period, W. George Beers. By profession he was a Montreal dentist, founder of the *Canada Journal of Dental Science,* the first dental journal in Canada; yet he found time to indulge his enthusiasm for all outdoor Canadian sports, summer and winter. He has been called "the father of lacrosse," as he was the first to reduce the game to a set of rules; and he organized in 1876 the first Canadian lacrosse team to visit the British Isles.

Beers wrote many articles and several books on Canadian sports, always in an engaging style. He criticized those who "coop themselves up, moping around the stove in winter, and making up their minds to be as disagreeable as possible." He urged everyone outdoors, to enjoy the health and excitement.

The "cousin" he speaks of was an American visitor; anyone from the United States was always called an "American cousin." The narrative appears in Beers's book *Over the Snow, or the Montreal Carnival* (Montreal, 1883) , pages 32, 35-37, 41-43.

We have had two days' suspicion of a thaw; the snow has sunken; when the wind changes, again, and a sharp frost sets in, the hills are in splendid order for tobogan-ing, and the moonlight "rolls through the dark blue depths," making the night as bright as day . . .

"Well, I must confess," says our irrepressible cousin, as he stands on the hill holding the leading-line of his tobogan, and studying the way they do it, "this sort of thing looks more like madness than method. There is a dare-devil sort of delight in it I like, though; so here goes for a trial."

Somehow or other, he has the look of one who is green in experience, and a Canadian friend offers to pilot him down. He seats himself in front, tucks his toes under the bend, and holds on by the leading-string; his friend gives it a shove, jumps on behind, steering with one foot, and away they go, the snow scared into maelstroms and whirlwinds about our cousin's face, — here shooting like lightning over glare ice, there leaping in the air as the tobogan bounds over a *cahot*, or ground-swell, and coming down flop, as if thrown from a catapult, as it lands on the level; now scudding away again in maddest velocity, a mile in a few seconds, the sport of the law of gravitation and a steep hill, our cousin's breath sometimes almost whisked out of his body, until he reaches the bottom, tobogan shaking, and he quaking, as if Death had had him by the shoulders, and had given him a rough shake. Yet he gets up, and finds that, unlike the traditional Turk, whose head had been severed with such nicety and sharpness, he can sneeze without losing his head, and, in fact, is more anxious to try again than to go home.

Côte des Neiges and McTavish's Hills, in my school-days, were the grand hills for toboganing in Montreal; but by and by the encroachments of building drove the toboganists to Brehaut's Hill and Clarke avenue at Côte St. Antoine, or to an open and more public space called Fletcher's Field. . . .

"Is there any real risk in toboganing?" Of course there is, and that's half the vim of it; but accidents happen in the best regulated sports. Three years ago one of our club was sliding down Brehaut's, when his tobogan bounced over a *cahot*. Down came the toboganist on the flat of his back in some mysterious way no one could understand, with a broken spine, and death before him in two weeks. Once I had a friend in the front seat of my tobogan backed by two ladies and myself. We were enjoying the sensation of running against a fence at the end of our descent, and I had warned him to keep in his legs, and not fear the concussion; but at once he thrust out his right leg, and got a compound fracture which laid him up for twelve weeks.

Toboganists are always bunting against something. It gets monotonous without an occasional upset, and if you cannot get them accidentally, half the fun is in making the sleigh swerve around when at top speed so as to get them on purpose. It's sometimes very sore when you make a sort of hop, skip and jump, over glare ice and a *cahot*, and rattle your bones almost out of joint as you come down with a crash. But there's no danger at all on a large hill without *cahots*, and not any anywhere if you are really careful. You'll get jolted and jerked, and covered with snow from head to toe, but that's healthy. But you'll get many a fascinating and thrilling ride without a single upset, and scarcely a joggle. It all depends on the condition of the hill, and the character of your steerer. I remember once coming down Côte des Neiges Hill, when at the bottom standing square in the way of crossing the street, was a *habitant's* horse and sleigh. A man stood on the road with his back to the hill, talking to the farmer. Two of us were on the tobogan, and within a few yards of the horse; the road was smooth ice. We both laid back our heads and like a flash shot under the belly of the horse between his legs. All we heard was a fierce neigh of fright from the horse. "If he had kicked?" It would have been bad for the horse, methinks.

The French writer Auguste Achintre wrote a lively account of the transformation that came over St. James Street on a Saturday afternoon in winter. Toward the end of the century Saturday had become a half-holiday, and as soon as the offices and workshops were closed, everyone seemed to head for St. James Street, to join the crowd and to see and be seen. The sidewalks could scarcely hold the full stream of people moving along.

This description pictures the profusion of furs that marked the Victorian era in Montreal, as may also be seen by reading the long advertisements of the fur shops. Furs were offered in amazing variety, and often at prices that most people could afford. Furs made the boots and the gloves, and not only the coats but the head-pieces.

A writer of grace and imagination, Auguste Achintre (1834-1886) was a frequent contributor to the periodicals of the time. He was born in Besançon, France, was educated at Aix-en-Provence and Paris, and came to Canada after spending five years in Haiti. He was successively editor of *Le Pays* and *L'Opinion Publique* in Montreal, and wrote two books, one on Quebec politics and one on St. Helen's Island. His description of St. James Street on a wintry Saturday afternoon is from his article "L'Hiver en Canada. La Rue St. Jacques à Montréal," in the issue of *Nouvelles Soirées Canadiennes*, Quebec, for November and December, 1883, pages 535-38, 541-45.

St. James Street's gala spectacle begins every Saturday afternoon in winter at two o'clock in the afternoon and ends at five. On that day the principal business houses, the banks, the Stock Exchange, the government departments and a great number of other establishments close their offices and their workshops for the afternoon. All their staff — high officials, employees and clerks, workers and managers — dressed up, combed, brushed, hatted, booted and gloved for the occasion, most of them accompanied by their wives and children, come to join the parade.

It is a sort of weekly Longchamps, where the ladies of fashion and the dandies give the tone and set the fashion of the season. . . .

Picture to yourself a double stream of people, flowing on each side of the street, a tide that almost overflows the sidewalks. People are marching abreast, in groups of three of four when they can, usually in twos, as in the ranks of a procession or convoy; or often, one after the other, like ducks on their way to the river. . . .

Greetings are exchanged in the American fashion, much more concise than the English would do: a gesture, a movement of the finger this way, a nod of the head, a slight bow that way, a wink to the right, a blink to the left, while saying "How are you?" on one side and *"Comment ça va?"* on the other, as the responses criss-cross. . . .

Next to the animation of the street, what is most surprising is the originality of the different head-gear, and the way all the many-coloured furs used in making the different kinds of Canadian winter overcoats glisten in the bright wintry sun.

Many are wearing cylindrical or pyramidal head-pieces, like travelling Persians. Others, adopting the rectangular lines of the policeman's helmet, wear their hats tipped over the ear, affecting the smartness of Hussar officers. There goes somebody with a Polish *schapska*. This one is wearing a square cap; that one has a judge's "toque"; quite a few have the tall Cossack hat, or the biretta of the old Doges, etc., etc.

An extraordinary effect is the contrast that every head-piece makes between the appearance and the social position of the owner, between seeming and being. For example, this gentleman, a quiet book-keeper, will take on the fierce look of a Hetman from the Ukraine. And this one here, a modest clerk, might be mistaken for a Margrave or a Boyard. This other one, a tall, thin church-warden of the parish, re-creates, with his white beard, an alchemist of the Middle Ages. That notary could pass for a Bulgar, and this druggist recalls the Emir of Caboul or the Khan of Bokara. You might imagine that the heads in this group had been taken from an Assyrian bas-relief, and these others are in the style of Memphis. Still others, with bands that encircle their skull-caps like the windings of a turban, and enveloped in their ulsters, remind you of the old men in fur overcoats whom the Flemish masters put in their pictures.

Except for the kind and quality of fur, the shape of women's head-wear is not very different. Picture in your mind a little cap *à la Buridan*, ornamented on one side, perhaps with a white eagle's plume, perhaps with a peacock's, sometimes a humming-bird's, most often with a marten's snout with enamel eyes — and imagine such a hat shoved against the chignon — and you will have a model head-piece of the fair sex. The feet and hands have as much finery as the head. The kid, the deer, the chamois, the dog — all have given their supple skins for women's foot-wear, which is then given an inner lining like birds' nests. The beaver, the seal, the moose give up their velvety skins for women's hands. The moose-skin gloves, when worn by the men, are veritable armlets; they cover the forearm and rise even above the elbow. . . .

It is sad to see that the old French-Canadian costume is being abandoned for the caprices of fashion. Very seldom do you see anyone wearing this outdated costume of the first French colonists. If you look hard enough, you may find a picturesque few still going by. To be precise, I see three young men dressed this way: short coat of chestnut-coloured coarse wool, blue-lined or gray, buttoning in front, with a hood behind. All three have their waists tightly wound three times with the *ceinture fléchée* of red silk, with the fringed ends hanging down one side. The notched embroidery on the collar, the piping on the seams and cuffs set off the colour of the cloth. The calves of their legs stand out in the ribbed worsted, held above the knee by garters. Round their legs are their mocassin thongs. Such clothing is light, comfortable and in good taste. But, unfortunately, it is to be had in any shop, and that seems to be reason enough for having nothing to do with it any more.

Montreal's Winter Carnivals had their origin in February, 1882. The "Tuques Bleues" of the Montreal Snowshoe Club were holding their annual meeting. Robert Davidson McGibbon, a twenty-four-year-old lawyer, was replying to the toast, "Our Winter Sports." The subject made him quickly eloquent, and he advanced a novel proposal.

Was it enough for Montrealers simply to enjoy the sports of their wonderful winters? Why should not all the clubs of the city unite in one great Winter Carnival? "Why not call in the world," he asked, "to see us as we are in all the gaiety and fervor of our mid-winter sports?"

The proposal was so interesting that it survived the summer. The next November a meeting to discuss it was held in the Windsor Hotel. McGibbon was elected chairman. George Iles, the manager of the Windsor, said he was certain raising the money would encounter no obstacles, for a Winter Carnival would bring a great deal of money into the city. The idea caught the imagination of Montrealers. Committees were appointed and in January, 1883, the first Winter Carnival took place.

The Winter Carnivals grew greater year by year, and visitors were drawn from many parts of the world. The Carnival of 1887 was described for English readers in *Murray's Magazine*. The anonymous writer pictures the tobboganing by electric light, and how the Jacques Cartier Slide (on Jacques Cartier Square, below Nelson's Monument) sent the toboggans shooting over the ice of the St. Lawrence. There was the Ice Palace on Dominion Square, the Fancy Dress Ball at the indoor Victoria Rink. Altogether, it was a "careless life and pleasure-seeking, a gay riot of fun and forgetfulness!"

This account of the Winter Carnival appeared in *Murray's Magazine* under the heading "Canadian Topics," May, 1887.

All sorts of festivity brightened the Carnival week and made it a great success. There were sleigh races and horse races; races on snow-shoes, on skates and in mocassins; slidings; concerts; processions; music; Lacrosse matches; fancy-dress skating balls; tandem drives, and a general roaming about through the snowy streets, of a pleasure-seeking crowd who seemed to be enjoying everything. Fifty thousand strangers came, it is said, to share the fun in our gay Northern city. Most popular were the toboggan slides, their gaunt wooden framework clothed with bright decoration of spruce boughs looped with festoons of red bunting and gay flags streaming aloft into the blue. Down their icy slopes dashed one toboggan after another (an official in authority on the top platform to prevent too quick succession) bearing tucked-up blanket-coated sliders clinging together as they raced past lines of gazing people and sped away, a flash of colour, far over the white frozen river below. One slide was seventeen hundred feet long, at an angle of one hundred and seventy-five feet. A pleasant sight at evening was the laughing crowd on this slide, who, between rows of brilliant electric lamps and gaudy streamers that danced in wintry wind, tore off amid ringing cheers, and dashed at a rate of seventy miles an hour down the steep, vanishing on the starlit plain far away!

Up on the "Mountain Park," among tossing pines, a roadway walled with snow led to another slide, near which stood a little club house of pine logs, bright with fire and lamplight, and gay with sound of revel — in strange contrast with the still white uplands without, down which the "shoot" went in terribly steep descent, plunging into a ravine over the brow of which glowed, like a sea of light, the well-lit streets of Montreal.

Very exciting was the Lacrosse match, played by men in closely-fitting Jersey suits, and on skates. Marvellous were their rapid flights and swift manœuvres, rushing hither and thither, more flying than skating — darting like the swallow, swooping like the gull — but always clutching their sticks or queer comma-shaped stringed bats, in pursuit of a small ball as it skimmed from end to end and side to side of the huge decorated rink, propelled by these bats in the skaters' efforts to take their opponents' goal. The goal consisted of two flags stuck on the ice at each end of the rink, and victory lay in sending the ball between the flags, when the imaginary garrison immediately capitulated. Sometimes a regular "scrimmage" would take place as the players battled, and then skates flashed and bats flew in a manner that looked, and indeed was, very dangerous; but the sound of music and cheers of spectators encouraged the combatants, who fought with such graceful vigour. The battle always ended bloodlessly, with a series of wonderful twistings and pirouettes on the part of all the skaters, both victors and vanquished.

But *the* feature of Carnival week was a large castellated building, surrounding fourteen thousand square feet of hard snow, and open to the sky. This "castle," of excellent proportions and of handsome form, with its battlemented and loopholed walls, its stately towers eighty to one hundred feet high, was made entirely of clear blocks of greenish ice, held firmly together by the freezing of water poured between the blocks. In starlight, sunlight, and electric light always beautiful, its delicately pure and lovely hues were radiant on the night of the storming and capture by a mock army of two thousand snow-shoers, who wound their way through the busy streets and the sixty thousand spectators congregated on Dominion Square to see the assault. From far up the mountain to which Montreal gracefully clings, these snow-shoe clubs, all in suits of gaily variegated blanket and coloured woollen caps, wearing snow-shoes and carrying high flaming torches, marched in procession, forming a long line of coloured light, from which glared incessantly the flash of rockets and Roman candles as the mimic army followed the slopes of Mount Royal and approached the castle. The "Tuque Bleu" Club, six hundred strong, the "Tuque Rouge," the "Trappeur," "Holly," "Nationale," "Emerald," and others, on they come, the brave music of a national Canadian air rising into the purple night sky. Ranged at last in battle array before the castle they demanded surrender, and from the castle turrets were boldly defied. Along the gleaming battlements, now illuminated by red fires within the enclosure, ran the besieged, making preparations for resistance. Up the winding icy stairways they could be seen through open loopholes as they mounted the towers, loaded with arms and ammunition consisting of nothing more dangerous than great bundles of fireworks.

On the bare and gleaming snow expanse round the castle the enemy was by this time busily forming for an assault, which opened presently after a fine blast of trumpets with a mighty cheer and dash. At the same instant lo! earth and sky blazed with flashings of light, red, blue, green, and yellow, as hundreds of rockets and Roman candles soared upwards and poured down again in streams of gorgeous fire. Away over the great stone city, snow-filled streets and ice-bound river, away up to the stars, sparkled a thousand moving colours. Night's silence echoed with shouts and cheers and counter cheers as the mock combatants pressed forward. Presently clouds of reddened smoke made weird and ghostly the moving crowd, and dimmed the fairy castle. The clustering figures on the battlements began to disappear. The cheers grew fainter, until at last as the enemy closed round the fortress with fresh shouts of victory and fresh salvos of artillery, the proud flag on topmost tower slowly drooped and disappeared. An exultant shout rose from the conquerors as they dashed forward, and the icy stronghold was captured at last!

This picture from the Middle Ages, in the frame of a new world, with ice for stone-work, blanket-coats for armour, and rockets for cross-bow and battle-axe, greatly delighted the masses, and for days afterwards crowds were to be seen gazing at the diamond-tinted castle which stood all unscathed, waiting for the gentle spring breathings before which alone its proud towers will fall.

One evening was devoted to a fancy-dress skating Carnival, and on this occasion half Montreal society died of envy, while the other half crammed the rink galleries and sat ten deep in spaces hardly large enough for five. The icy flooring was quite deserted when they first assembled, shining in strong electric light, and shaded by crimson flags. A miniature lighthouse, all ice and snow, with a revolving light flashing through coloured glass panes, was planted in the centre. . . . a hundred skaters in fancy costume of every colour and variety darted simultaneously on to the ice from some mysterious regions beneath the galleries where they had been quietly assembling. In a moment the scene flashed with bounding life and gaiety, as the bewildering crowd, to the time of rapid music, flew round the rink, a very halo of brilliant colour — peasants, courtiers, cow-boys, matadors, angels, fishwomen, empresses, fairies and tambourine girls, hand in hand with Mother Hubbard and Moonlight, Mephistopheles, Portia, Juliet, Joan of Arc, and the Evening Star — a Carnival indeed of careless life and pleasure-seeking, a gay riot of fun and forgetfulness!

In the eighteen-eighties a change was coming over the face of Montreal. The city was moving into the office age — a movement that has continued till today. Previously offices had been relatively small, and were built by companies for their own use only. But with the growth of Canadian corporations with headquarters in Montreal, offices assumed a new architectural grandeur. And office buildings as such, where various companies could rent space, began to make their appearance.

Examples of the new, large corporation offices were the New York Life Insurance Company's building on the east side of Place d'Armes, at the corner of St. James Street, and the Canadian Pacific Railway's new office on Windsor Street; and an example of the new office buildings for general purposes was the Temple Building, erected by the corporation of St. James Methodist Church on the site of the old St. James

Street church, near St. Peter Street, after the congregation had moved to the great "Methodist Cathedral" on St. Catherine.

An anonymous writer of 1889 believed that quite apart from the nature of the new demand, architecture in Montreal was breaking away from the restricted concepts of the past and was entering a new and better era. The feeling for beautiful materials, for graceful lines, and "the use of ornament that is not tawdry" was transforming the city.

This writer also saw a new era of grander residences, or at least of grand residences in a new and purer style. He had high praise for the mansion Senator George A. Drummond was building on the south-east corner of Sherbrooke and Metcalfe Streets. He also foresaw a time when not only offices but fine residential buildings would be erected, in which each tenant could rent space. These apartment buildings, which he still called "tenements," were bound to come, though not much of artistic value had as yet made its appearance.

The article, possibly written by an architect, was entitled "The Evolution of Montreal," and appeared in *The Witness Carnival Number*, Montreal, February 4-9, 1889. The typographical errors (including some in punctuation) have been left uncorrected.

That there has been such an extension and modification of the conditions affecting and controlling the growth of Montreal within such a recent period as to bring to pass really a new architectural era, may be under all circumstances too bold a generalization; but it seems justified if not proved by the difference in the purposes, structures and ornamentation of the principal buildings, both commercial and residential, which have been erected during the past few years. That there has been a substantial change in the commercial status of Montreal, — caused primarily by the wide expansion of the area subsidiary in a commercial sense to the city, and secondly by the causes that have made her an industrial and financial as well as a commercial centre, — cannot be gainsaid.

That such a change has been produced in Montreal, the great demand for offices, — which has so powerfully affected the building market that with one or two exceptions every important commercial structure erected for some years past in the heart of the city has almost as a matter of course been exclusively devoted to supplying this demand, — offers abundant proof. This fact goes but a small way, however, towards justifying the more general conclusion that a new era has been begun. It is in the character, not the purposes; in the architectural intent and methods, not in the actual results achieved, not only in the new commercial but in the new architectural structures, — that the proof of the wider generalization is to be sought. Among the new commercial buildings of Montreal there are four, — the great office buildings erected by the Standard Insurance Company, the New York Life Insurance Company, the corporation of the old St. James Street Methodist Church, and the Canadian Pacific Railway Company, — which, from their size, cast, and the purposes they are intended to fulfil, have no compeers in the Montreal which for the sake of comparison may be called "old."

Three of these buildings, the Standard, New York Life, and Methodist building, stand upon one street, within a stone's throw of each other; their purpose is the same, and there has been no stint of money upon any of them. They are emphatically different in design, but all agree in this, the use of a material in itself beautiful, and susceptible of beautiful treatment, in substantial truth of material throughout, and in the use of ornament that is not tawdry. It was in these very points that old Montreal was deplorably deficient.

The new station and general offices of the Canadian Pacific is in many respects one of the most interesting buildings in the city. In it the common grey limestone of Montreal has been used with a truer perception of its character as a building material and with better effect than ever before. It has been given a texture which not only prevents it from being unpleasantly cold but is admirably suited to the size and power of the building it composes. Not only have the laws of the truth of material been implicitly followed in this building but, with the exception of the lintels of the lower story, which are carried by flat brick arches, it is constructively true, and variety of effect and artistic unity have been secured without distorting the construction.

As these great office buildings were erected to supply a special demand, and are of a special class, their superiority to the less pretentious commercial buildings of a former period, taken by itself, would prove but little. There has been, however, a corresponding improvement in the architecture of the warehouses erected late, In material, in ornament, and in structural form. such buildings as the Robertson or Wilson blocks on Craig street are very much superior to the older order of commercial building. That this improvement is uniform is unfortunately not the case witness certain incongruous combinations erected on Great St. James street this very year: but it is sufficiently uniform to create as a whole a substantial improvement in the appearance of the commercial parts of the city.

The conditions affecting the construction of residences, both small and great, have been as materially changed during the last few years as those controlling commercial erections, but by other causes. The increase in population and wealth has played, of course, an important part, but it has been in another direction. On the one hand, the increase in wealth, or rather the increase in the number of wealthy men, has caused the erection of quite a number of very large and expensive houses; on the other, the increase in population, and therefore of the value of land, has led up to the development of what we called "tenements," and of great numbers of terraces of "cottages."

The architectural features of mansion, tenement and cottage alike, have been much affected by the revival in architecture in the United States and in Europe, and by a better knowledge of the effect of the climate upon buildings, and, let it be hoped, by a truer and more general conception of the elements that make a house beautiful. The building which proves beyond question how great the advance in architecture as an art has been in Montreal is the house which is being erected at the corner of Sherbrooke and Metcalf streets for Senator Drummond. This beautiful house is still in such an uncompleted state, at the time of writing, as to make a study of it as a whole impossible, for it is to be enriched by a wealth of carving and ornament, every detail of which has been thought out by the architect with as much care as if he were working out his ideal in marble instead of sandstone. The general design of the house is strong and good. The strong corner tower, which is still the tower of a house not of a fortress, and the two gables rising steeply to the grotesque "beastes" that terminate them, produce a most admirable effect in the mass. The material of the two street fronts of the house is a very rich and beautifully textured sandstone, and not only are capital and panel to be richly carved, but these belts of carven ornament are to sweep about the house; and richly carved and ornamented porch, oriel window, and balcony, add beauty and expansion to the whole.

Besides this grandly artistic house, even stronger evidences of the new era are to be found in the great number of very beautiful sandstone and brick, and sandstone, brick and terra cotta houses, which are neither large nor costly, and the most of which have been built within the last year or two.

So far nothing very beautiful in the shape of "tenements," that is a double terraced house, or "cottages," a two storied self contained terrace house, has been produced; but out of all the experimenting that is now going on something is sure to come. In ecclestiastical architecture the great "Methodist Cathedral," the grand new church the St. James Street congregation have erected for themselves on St. Catherine street, is the chief event so far of the new era. St. Peter's Cathedral is, however, yearly taking shape, and let him who doubts that there is really an architectural view, that is a view depending for its beauty upon architectural effect solely, glance up Little St. Antoine street from St. James street, and see the grand Dome of St. Peter's closing up the vista made by clustering roofs and a street picturesque in its slovenliness.

The theme of Montreal's "two solitudes" found one of its most forceful expressions in the nineteenth century in an article by C. H. Farnham published in 1889. Montreal, he said, was a house divided against itself. That this divided house not only managed somehow to stand but to grow was a marvel; but it grew from "the separate, not the united, efforts of the races." In other words, it grew in spite of itself, and the ultimate danger in its divided state remained.

Other writers of the nineteenth century had written of the city's racial divisions. Thomas Storrow Brown, in his account of Montreal in the early years of the century, had dwelt upon them. But Farnham's article is remarkable for approaching the problem less in the mood of political partisanship, or commercial annoyance, or appreciation of quaint contrasts, than in a sociological spirit.

A writer with so incisive an approach is far removed from most of those who saw in Montreal's divided condition only contrasts that heightened the city's interest. Farnham saw these divisions as far too deep and ominous to be accepted as merely picturesque.

This remarkable analysis appeared in *Harper's New Monthly Magazine*, June, 1889. The selection here given is from pages 84-5, 90-91, 94-5, 98.

Montreal is a striking exception to the text that a house divided against itself cannot stand. Its divisions are so fundamental and persistent that they have not diminished one iota in a century, but rather increased. The two irreconcilable elements are Romanism and Protestantism; the armies are of French and English blood. The outlook for peace is well-nigh hopeless, with two systems of education producing fundamental differences of character, and nourishing religious intolerance, race antipathy, social division, political antagonism, and commercial separation.

Nevertheless, this city of disunion flourishes as the green bay-tree, with a steady if not an amazing growth, which is due chiefly to the separate, not the united, efforts of the races. . . .

The population comprises three race divisions — the English-speaking Scotch, English, Irish, and Americans; the French Canadians; and a few mixed families of English and French. Foreigners are almost unknown in Montreal, if the Americans be excepted. The community or society in general has no clearly defined castes. What aristocracy there was disappeared with the garrison; and as English aristocratic manners and customs seem ill adapted to this commercial community, all attempts in this direction have failed. Society thus lacks the order and power that may be derived from large homogeneous divisions; unhappily it suffers, as many other communities do, from the pettiness of small divisions or cliques. The ultrafashionable set changes *personnel* rather rapidly, with the changes of wealth, but preserves enough leaven of polish from decade to decade to raise the material. The national character and many homes well furnished in the English style give to the city a delightful air of comfort, cheerfulness, and solidity. One of the largest and most important social elements of Montreal are the professors of McGill University. The Americans, about one hundred families, are not a prominent element in fashionable life. The Scotch are easily the leading people here, as they are so generally in British colonies. And the Irish fill here their customary industrial and political rôles, generally in peace and order, but now and then with an Orange riot or some outbreak of hatred against the French Canadians. . . .

The French Canadian upper classes are in a singular social condition. They form a society that is mature, being the product of an old and complete system of education, laws, language, customs, and religion. They are gregarious by nature, and given to social enjoyments; they are naturally a capable race; they have always been most closely united in national interests and sympathy, and opposed to internal variations in culture as well as to external influences; and they have, relatively to the cost of their education and their living, always been sufficiently well-to-do to command what education their Church chose to give. It is true that the conquest deprived the national life of most of its seigneurs and leaders of society, and that the old families since then have died out or sunk into the ranks. But these misfortunes merely changed the *personnel* of society from the titled to the professional class, which, if more democratic, is also more numerous and active. Courtliness of manners undoubtedly declined; but the institutions of learning were in no way disturbed; the religious, moral, and intellectual forces and interests and tendencies were not changed. The race has increased wonderfully in numbers and power and means of culture; and it seems probable that society has grown with the growth of the country to be both larger and more cultivated than it was before the conquest. And as to keeping steadfastly to its characteristics, so faithfully have the French Canadian Roman Catholic manners, customs, traditions, education, language, laws, domestic life, social unity, been preserved that the race is a marvel to all visitors. It seems, then, not unjust to say that French Canadian society is quite mature, sufficiently numerous, and in native capacity able to sustain a social life of varied interests and elevating efforts. The surprise is therefore great to find the society of this largest and most wealthy of French Canadian communities almost without social organization, lacking social leaders, amusements of worth, intellectual, scientific, and artistic centres and activities. Doubtless the lack of large fortunes and some other material circumstances may have contributed somewhat to this result; but it cannot be doubted that the chief cause is the fact that the civilization of the French Canadian people is to such an extent moulded and restricted by its religious guardians. . . .

Montreal is divided sharply into two parts, the French and the English, the East and the West ends. In each part the business portion lies near the river, the wealthier homes near the mountain. In the poorer French region the signs, the trades, the domestic life, the houses, are all distinctly French and quite Continental in character. The streets have lines of small houses of one or one and a half stories, with dormer-windows peeping out of steep roofs, and here and there a little nich of a piazza; a lane now and then gives some shadowy and broken forms and quiet nooks. But all unity and effectiveness are lost by the presence of many modern houses utterly plain and ungracious.

The chief business streets of the city — St. James, Notre Dame, McGill — give a good impression by their massive limestone buildings, both public and commercial. Here and there in the town is met a touch of grace and beauty, as in the English cathedral and the Chapel of Notre Dame de Lourdes. The cut-stone residences along Sherbrooke and other streets at the foot of the mountain embody well the leading tones of the English life here — solidity, comfort, and cheerfulness. But you feel everywhere that Montreal is distinctly a Northern city: the winter predominates; the best life is within, both in character and in architecture.

Naturally enough the most interesting features of the city to an American visitor thus strolling about are those connected with the leading element of the French Canadian life — those of the Roman Catholic religion. Here, among a Roman Catholic population noted chiefly for their lack of wealth, is building a cathedral one-third the size of St. Peter's, and of the same shape, excepting that this one has a pointed roof to shed snow. They have already, besides many other churches, the great Notre Dame, the largest in America excepting the cathedral of Mexico. It seats 10,000 people, and will hold 15,000. The official poster at the door asserts that the great bell in the tower is the largest in the world. It is [really] the eighth bell in size, weighing only 24,780 pounds. In the interior, vast but somewhat harsh and gaudy, you may see an ornate spiral pulpit and a bronze statue of St. Peter, of which the toes are well polished. You may continue visiting churches and chapels all day. None of them contain any art of importance, but they reveal a religious life of the Middle Ages kept up with marvellous force in this nineteenth century. One of the pleasantest scenes of this religious life may be witnessed in the city of the dead. In the cemetery on the mountain, along the street of tombs, are erected little grottoes, each having in colored alto-rilievo a tableau of the stations of the cross. A priest leads slowly the flock from station to station, and explains to the kneeling people the dogmatic value of the sufferings portrayed. The trees, birds, chants, sunshine, and the murmuring winds all combine to make the ceremony touching. The route ends on a knoll where three huge crosses and figures represent most realistically the final agony. When I visited the place, of a fine June day, a company of convent girls and nuns were holding a merry picnic at this place. After their picnic they knelt for prayer, and then drove away rejoicing. On many of the graves are evidences of tender regard for the departed — little plaster statues of saints, photographs of the deceased, or little altars with candles and crucifixes, set up in glass-covered little boxes or toy chapels. . . .

Montreal seems to be full of gigantic monasteries. . . . As the population of the city is divided as to religion, the place has a duplicate of nearly every kind of chartitable institution, besides a great number of churches. Probably the chief obstruction to the city's growth is this ecclesiastic element. I was told that about twenty per cent. of the property pays no taxes; many religious corporations manufacture various articles and make a ruinous competition with the working classes; and much of the land is locked up in religious orders that will neither sell nor improve it. . . .

The French Canadian merchant does not hold a commanding position commercially. French Canadians themselves prefer to deal with English houses and to work for English employers. In the entire province scarcely a French Canadian has ever organized an important successful enterprise; lumbering, wholesale trade, public works, are almost invariably in other hands.

9

Nostalgic Memories of the Nineties

In the early eighteen-nineties a trip to Greene Avenue on the horse-car could be "quite an adventure" for a child. It was the end of the line, and though a cluster of houses stood in the neighbourhood, it was still out in the country, where strawberries could be picked in the fields.

Obviously the horse-cars, slow as they were, had something of the satisfaction of simplicity, when power was still being provided visibly by the horse, and when movement was at a horse's speed, as since the days of the Roman Empire and earlier. It is said that walking was nearly as fast as going by horse-car, the advantage of the cars being a certain amount of shelter from the rain or snow. They were not greatly used, for in the small, compact city most people walked to work, to the shops and to church. Others had their own stables behind their houses, or hired cabs.

L. H. D. Sutherland describes what travel by the horse-cars was like. His description is reproduced here from manuscript reminiscences, which were first published in the historical column "All Our Yesterdays," in *The Gazette,* Montreal, April 27, 1957.

In the early 1890's it was customary for the nurse **to**

take the younger children for a walk in the afternoon to give them the sun and air. We often walked to Dominion Square, where our nurse had many friends and we were free to enjoy ourselves playing with the other children.

Dominion Square at that time had no statues, only a few benches and the two guns standing on the south side of Dorchester Street. The first statue was Sir John A. Macdonald, the Father of Confederation, which we saw being set in place.

As a great treat, we were occasionally taken on a picnic and always to the same spot — this was Greene Ave. at the corner of St. Catherine St., where we picked strawberries in the fields and had such refreshments as are usually served at picnics. To mark the occasion we often had a bottle of Gurd's sweet ginger ale, which was declared delicious, even though when taken too quickly it re-acted in a somewhat juvenile manner.

Transportation to Greene Ave. was quite an adventure, and this was accomplished in the street car of the day. This was open all down one side, with benches running crosswise. The conductor moved back and forth on a step running the length of the car, collecting the fares, which were in cash.

At intervals he pulled a cord which registered the fares on an indicator at the end of the car. As the cord was pulled so rapidly it was next to impossible to count the number of fares recorded, and it was commonly thought that he collected somewhat more cash than was recorded.

Eventually a more efficient system was installed and the poor conductor's earnings were then limited to his salary. This setback was serious but gossip relates that many were able to augment their income by working after hours for the operators of card games, where the fact that "Quickness of the Hand Deceives the Eye" is very much to the benefit of the proprietor.

If one thinks that the lot of the conductor was a very unhappy one, please take a look at the driver. The cars ran on steel rails and were drawn by a pair of farm horses, who progressed at about five miles per hour, exclusive of the time lost to load and discharge the patrons.

Superficially this would appear quite satisfactory, if one neglected to take into account that, when the horses stopped, the car naturally continued on its way, due to its momentum. As Lord Rutherford taught the students at McGill University, momentum is the weight of the object multiplied by its speed. Although the speed was not excessive, the weight of the car was considerable and it was quite obvious that if the horses stopped, the momentum was suddenly and unpleasantly increased.

In view of the above, it was obvious that the speed of the car must be regulated, so that it came to a stop at the same time as the horses. This was accomplished by means of a hand-brake operated by the driver, who diligently turned a handle which regulated the speed of the car, and in view of the many stops and starts he was fully occupied throughout the trip.

The management, after due consideration, decided to extend the system up Park Ave., and the rails were duly fixed in place.

However, at the official opening, it soon became evident that a pair of horses could not pull a loaded car up the hill of Bleury St. to Sherbrooke St. To solve the problem a third horse was stationed at the bottom of the hill, and with this added assistance the ascent of the hill was laboriously accomplished.

No provision was made to turn the cars when they reached the end of the rails. It was therefore necessary to unhitch the horses and drive them to the other end of the car, where they were duly attached and proceeded on the return journey.

The Street Railway having overcome the initial difficulties somewhat successfully, were now faced with a more serious problem.

The franchise from the Ville de Montreal called for year round operation. In view of the fact that no effort was made to remove snow from the streets, and, furthermore, that the bordering landowners were called on by law to keep their sidewalks clear of snow, which was done by shovelling the snow onto the roadway, it was quite obvious that the cars could not run on the rails in wintertime.

After considerable thought and discussion, it was decided that sleighs must be used. This meant that the poor horses in the wintertime were hitched to a heavy sleigh and proceeded to render an even slower service than in the summer.

The type of sleigh selected was what is known as a Kingfisher, which is a long sleigh with two seats facing each other and running the full length of the vehicle.

Imagine the difficulty of entry and exit when one had to walk over the feet of the seated passengers, as the only point of exit was the rear. For warmth, the floor was covered with straw, and horse-blankets were provided as some protection. This was no expense to the shareholders, as the blankets were not required when the horses were at work.

Later, when electricity became available, the Company arranged for plows and sweepers to clear the tracks and the poor horses were supposed to be pensioned, but it is to be feared many were sold.

With the advent of the electric car there was still the problem of heating. This was accomplished by a very small coal stove near the entrance at the rear. As it naturally required constant stoking, the conductor was under a continual barrage from the passengers to add more fuel.

A description of sport at the turn of the century is characteristically called "Muscular Montreal." It reviews the wide range of sport in the city, from the snowshoers climbing Mount Royal in the wintry moonlight, their beards heavy with frost, to the yachtsmen in summer in their twenty-footers on Lake St. Louis, defying the yachtsmen of the United States to win back the Seawanhaka Cup.

In the first half of the century curling, hunting and fishing, horse-racing, and fox-hunting were established. But after 1850 sport broadened out from the recreation of groups into becoming part of the whole scene, a matter of general pride and interest.

Professionalism in sport was shunned; only baseball was played for money. All other sports were played with no aim except physical development and skill and zest in contest. The amateur standards were exacting. Many young men got up for exercise before going to work, and work in those days began early; and the newcomer to any club soon found that the established members set him a hard pace.

This anonymous article appears in the later editions of *Illustrated Montreal. The Metropolis of Canada,* originally published in Montreal in 1890 by J. McConniff, who had his ticket agent's office in the Windsor Hotel. The following excerpt is from pages 65-77.

Every progressive country has its own way of developing the physique of its citizens. Germany and France teach them to play at soldiering; in Canada every man is or has been an athlete, which accounts for the stalwart handsome men for which Montreal in particular is noted. This love of muscular exertion is in the Canadian's blood, and the rotation of the seasons affords such change of sport, as to prevent any one sport from palling. He changes from blanket suit to flannel with the course of the sun, and from bathing dress to huge fur coat, and the den of a young Canadian is usually an arsenal of weapons with which he does more than merely kill time. The Canadian, and consequently the Montreal woman is only a degree behind her brother in this love of sport. She will be found reclining in the canoe he is paddling, she will walk long miles with him upon the snowshoe tramp, she adores the golfstick, and her cheeks flush over tennis. From even the more methodical work of the gymnasium she does not shrink, and she shows it in her graceful carriage, healthy color and rounded form.

Professionalism is almost unknown in the sporting world of Montreal, the baseball team being the only salaried players of any important game. This sport was introduced in 1897 and has magnificent grounds at the corner of St. Catherine street and Atwater avenue, just within the limits of the suburban town of Westmount. . . .

Immediately behind the "Windsor" is the celebrated Victoria Skating Rink, one of the finest in the world. Here will be found a happy crowd, gliding about on polished blades, over a magnificent sheet of ice. Hundreds are on the ice — some waltzing, some speeding swiftly round and round, and others performing the graceful evolutions of finished skaters. Hundreds more throng the spacious promenade, from which vantage ground they study the poetry of motion as exemplified by a world's champion, or a number of experts of both sexes, in what is undeniably one of the most beneficial of exercises and the most graceful known. Judged fairly, the ladies are certainly the better skaters. The majority of the gentlemen skate well, 'tis true, but only a small number are really experts, *i.e.,* capable of performing difficult figures with ease and grace. Yet one may see a waltz or quadrille danced upon this treacherous footing to perfection. The visitor is particullarly fortunate if opportunity is afforded for a sight of one of the grand fancy dress gatherings which are held a couple of times every winter at this rink or others. . . .

A hockey match at the "Arena," between any two of the prominent teams of the country, will also greatly interest all admirers of manly skill. Only good skaters and men of nerve can excel in it, for it frequently necessitates rough, fast and long-continued work. Swift skating, lightning turns, and close, hard checking of opponents, are essential to success, and good judgment and a well-controlled temper are needful qualifications. Falls are frequent naturally, but it is seldom any serious damage results, and the game is very exciting, commanding audiences of many thousands.

There are many other rinks in the city, some devoted principally to skating, where the fancy dress entertainments are only second to those at the Victoria, and where a number of important hockey matches are decided. Others again are the centres where prominent curling matches are held, and at these the visitor many glean, from the noise of the captains and the shouting, the savor of haggis and greens, etc., how strong is the Scottish element among the leading men of Montreal.

One of the most influential of organizations of its nature in America is the Montreal Amateur Athletic Association, which embraces in its large membership the best young men of the city, and exercises a marked influence in social life. The handsome stone structure, forming the headquarters of the M.A.A.A., is situated on Mansfield street, and here will be found all the latest and best appliances for the development of the muscles. Every purely amateur sport is encouraged, and, as most of the leading clubs in all branches of sport have been affiliated to the M.A.A.A., it is a strongly representative organization and a model of its kind. The beautiful grounds of the association are located in Westmount. They occupy a most advantageous site, and are surpassed by few, if any, rivals. The grounds of the Shamrock Lacrosse Club are at the other end of the city, and upon those two roomy squares of close green turf are fought out the championship games of lacrosse. Both grounds have a fine cinder track, club rooms, etc., and in the season an immense crowd sees the decision of championship amateur athletic events, and, not unfrequently, some genuine record-smashing.

Snowshoeing justly ranks among the leading pastimes. A tramp over the mountain, with say the merry men of St. George upon a moonlight night, will not soon be forgotten. Shoes are donned at the head of Peel street, and the pace-maker leads the way, followed by from twenty to fifty blanket-garbed "knights" in Indian file. Last of all comes the "whipper-in," whose duty is to look after tyros at the sport, and keep laggards to the pace. Through the snowy woods, they climb up the mountain side, the trees casting

weird black shadows over the spotless snow. "Click-clack!"
"click-clack!" sound the shoes in regular beat, every man
sticking to his work and holding his place in the long line
as best he may. Now they defile into an open space, and
the moon shines bright upon the royal purple and crimson
colors of the club. Beards are heavy with frost, and the
breath shows like steam in this keen night air, and they
form a charmingly picturesque band as they trudge
steadily along. Away below, the moon's rays flash upon
soaring spires and snow-laden roofs, and lower yet the
countless lights of the great city complete an effect that
is magical in its strange beauty. Now they enter the gloomy
pines and are lost to view in the velvet blackness of shadows the moon cannot penetrate, emerging lower down in
sight of the tinted lights of St. George's Club House. Soon
the pace quickens, the leader breaks into a run, and takes
his men right merrily along until the door of the club-
house is reached. "All up?" he shouts, and the trampers
reply, then shoes are taken off, and all prepare for an
evening's fun in the true snowshoer's style.

The beautiful club-house is admirably suited for its
purpose: its spacious ball-room will accommodate all probable visitors of a club whose membership numbers close
to five hundred, and in it the trampers soon assemble,
with others who, perhaps, have driven out from the city.
The senior officer of the club present acts as master of
ceremonies, the club pianist takes his position at the instrument, and a varied programme of songs, dances, reci-
tations and specialties is gone through — the club posses-
sing a surprising amount of talent in this direction. If
strangers are present, or it is the first appearance of new
members, the "bouncing contingent" are called upon, and

seize their victim and toss him aloft amid laughter and fun again and again, catching him safely, at each descent, in strong hands. At half past ten, all join in singing the national anthem, and the regular proceedings close. Volunteers may now be called upon, and the fun, perhaps, prolonged for an hour more, when word is passed round to prepare for home. The same style of amusement is also followed at other rendezvous.

If Montreal is the home of winter sports unique upon this continent, she is none the less the home of pastimes that depend not upon chill blasts, frozen streams and winding snow. She possesses the original hunt club of America, with magnificent kennels and club-house behind the mountain, and her red-coated horsemen hunt real foxes on their native heath. Many a glorious run is had in the season, and the hunt breakfasts are events of primary importance in the social set.

Another highly social amusement is found at the Racquet Court, built at a heavy expense and patronized by a large number of the "smart set."

But it is on the lake front, a few miles from Montreal, on Lake St. Louis, that Montrealers enjoy their summer sports most freely. Here are to be found the Bel-Air race track, the Forest and Stream Club, and the Royal St. Lawrence Yacht Club, and, clustered around these, or spread upwards for over twenty miles to Ste. Anne and Vaudreuil, are costly summer houses, in front of which springs at anchor the launch or the sailing yacht. Lake St. Louis has an enviable reputation for the number and speed of its twenty-footers, and for some years United States yachtsmen have vainly endeavored to win back the Seawanhaka Cup, won by G. Herrick Duggan from one of their crack racers. On Lake St. Louis, every Saturday during the season, there is almost certain to be a regatta at one of the resorts, which are distant from one another seldom more than two miles, and the scene is gay with lake craft of all kinds, pretty women and athletic men.

At these regattas the canoe races, particularly the races of the war-canoes, are always popular.

In summer, the whole city seems to turn amphibian. Even little children along the lake shore have their "punts" in which they paddle about, heedless of danger, while their elders as a rule care but little, so far as fear is concerned, which side of their yacht is uppermost, or whether they are in the water or not.

In the neighborhood of Dorval are the golf links which are reputed among the best in America, and greatly patronized.

At Ste. Rose, St. Lambert, Chambly, Longueuil, Boucherville, Laprairie, the Back River, and at dozens of other suburban resorts, Montrealers enjoy the summer months, yet leave enough in the city to crowd the grand stands when a lacrosse or base-ball game is in progress.

There is probably no game in the world quite as skillful as lacrosse. It is the historic game of Canada, to which Pontiac gave a terrible significance during his revolt. To those unaccustomed to the game, it is a most wonderful sight to see what clever players can do with these "sticks" in the matter of catching, holding and throwing the ball. Many of the league games of Canada are played in Montreal, and are attended by thousands. . . .

Montreal is the starting point for a large number of fine shooting and fishing tours, and the game laws of the province are not severe. The distance to good grounds is comparatively short, and as a consequence a large number of citizens avail themselves of their opportunity, particularly upon a holiday.

A special nostalgia belongs to the late-Victorian childhood. It was set (for the fortunate) in an opulent age, with all its discomforts and limitations encompassed by ease and interest. The mood may seem all the deeper in looking back because it was a world about to crash and disappear. The earlier Victorian period was one of struggle and striving; and though the end of the century was also in active motion, it yet had a sense of pause, a satisfied resting, a sort of timeless poise. Nor is this mood only in the retrospect. The literature of the time, its art and architecture, the very setting and way of life, seemed to dwell in a supreme sense of achievement and security, at least for those in a position to live in its big and ornate houses and to enjoy the round of social pleasures.

A picture of a girlhood in that late-Victorian Montreal, retrospective yet sharp and defined, was written by Mrs. Florence Mary Ramsden. The discomforts of fashion and custom are described, but the compensations lay in the more direct sense of things — the warmth of stoves, the smell of Demerara sugar in the cellar, the cries of the street-hawkers, the flash of the tandem clubs on a winter's day. Even the customs held intrusion at bay: communication by notes and not by telephone, the leaving of visiting cards, birth and death at home.

These reminiscences are reproduced from Mrs. Ramsden's manuscript, which was first published in the historical column "All Our Yesterdays" in *The Gazette*, Montreal, March 12, 1955.

"No, I never wore hoops but I did wear a bustle!" But more of that anon.

One of my earliest recollections is when I was about five years old my little brother and I used to hide behind the voluminous folds of my aunt's hoops when my father came at five o'clock to take us home to tea. We were blissfully unconscious that although our heads were covered, important parts of our anatomy were plainly visible. These hoops were very handy, for when my aunt came to dine at our house she pinned her cap of fine lace with pink or lavender ribbons to the wires, where it travelled in perfect safety.

No frilled or dainty organdy or nylon lingerie graced my childhood. Garments were strong, practical and unlovely — red flannel bloomers in winter, and in summer always a white flannel petticoat, with wide white cotton drawers and a many tucked white petticoat edged with embroidery.

Young girls rarely had fur coats (except the little ones in white rabbit coats and caps) but were smothered up in woollen "clouds," which got very wet with their frozen breath and caused many chapped chins. My first attempt at knitting was making garters for my mother (elastic being considered injurious for married ladies, stopping the circulation). These garters were about an inch wide and a yard long, made of soft white wool and I expect they were pretty grubby before they were finished.

There were few furnaces in those days in private houses, but we had a large friendly hall stove with mica windows which gave out a warm rosy glow. It had a protecting wire guard on which we hung our wet mitts and clouds. Gas was the universal illuminant and was very impure, burning with a blue flame and hissing a great deal and frequently freezing in very cold weather, when it had to be thawed out with methylated spirits. Many dinner parties were spoiled by the gas failing and candles having to be pressed into the service.

Every evening we children used to flatten our noses on

the window pane and watch the lamplighter with his magic wand sparking the lamps all up and down the street. Wooden pavements in all the residential districts gave place later to flag stones very badly laid and often tilted up by the frost. Each householder shovelled his own sidewalk and made a sorry job of it. Some scraped to the boards and others left hummocks of snow piled beside the road, often so high that a horse and sleigh were not visible from the walk, but these banks of snow were splendid to slide down or plunge through and get thoroughly wet!

Milk was delivered in large five-gallon cans and poured into the receptacle left on the doorstep or in the porch. It was eight cents a quart and knew nought of pasteurization or homogenizing. According to ritual, Candlemas Day "put the candles and the candle-sticks away," and our old cook, who was with us for 18 years, insisted on the kitchen tea for the maids without candles on Feb. 2nd.

Of course, there were no frigidaires in those days, and the ice-man just shot a 10 or 20 lb. block on to the pavement, unless you could bribe him to carry it in to the refrigerator. Fresh vegetables were rare in winter and canned goods unknown, but in our cellar we had big bins of potatoes, turnips, onions, carrots and very coarse cabbage. I still can see in the cool larder the curls of butter scooped from the 20 lb. tinnet (covered with a clean salted white cloth) and smell again the delicious Demerara sugar, and the barrel of white sugar, and the big packages of raisins, currants and spices.

Apples were plentiful and we had figs, dates and prunes and occasionally oranges and Malaga grapes. There was a new fruit imported — a shaddock — forerunner of the grapefruit, but very sour. Pineapples were a rare treat and bananas seldom seen. It is hard to believe that a lemon squeezer did not exist and the Dover egg-beater and mincing machine came later. The rubber hot water bottle came as a boon and a blessing to replace the brown stone bottles (originally containing gin from Holland) wrapped in flannel, which though warm, were very unyielding bedfellows!

The birth of a baby always took place in the parents' home and never in a sterilized maternity hospital ward, likewise when a death occurred the funeral took place from the residence and not from an undertaker's. A black streamer of crepe was nailed to the front door for an old person, tied with white ribbon for a younger, and pure white for a child. The hearses had plumes to correspond with the age of the deceased.

To return to things sartorial. . . . "Yes, I wore a bustle!" It was generally a small mattress-like affair stitched to my skirt, or a curious spiral contraption of two coils of wire attached to a stout piece of belting with a steel buckle, such as men have on their belts! The bustle was supposed to give a graceful sloping line to the long skirts, which were often four yards wide and faced (in the case of street dresses) with brush binding or bias velveteen — excellent carriers of dust and germs.

Zippers were quite unknown, and snap fasteners, and I remember a dress I had made in London which had 52 hooks and eyes. Evening dresses were laced up the back and necessitated someone sitting up till all hours of the night (or morning) to set you free. Black stockings were almost universal, cashmere for winter, open-work lisle thread or silk for summer and parties, but when brown shoes were not considered "too vulgar," ladies' stockings to match came in. Button boots were the fashion, but as I skated a great deal I wore trim laced boots made to order.

It was not until 1900 that we had a telephone. My father would not have his privacy invaded by any Tom, Dick or Harry ringing up at any hour of the day or night, consequently innumerable little notes had to be written for invitations and acceptances, and formal calls paid.

Every lady had an "At Home" day — 1st and 3rd Wednesday, or 2nd and 4th Thursday, and this meant leaving engraved cards for each adult member of the family and for any resident guest. At the end of the afternoon you found your card tray piled high with pasteboard. New Year's Day was the great day for gentlemen to visit; ladies stayed at home and dispensed sherry and cake from 11 in the morning till seven p.m.

Very popular were the Saturday Teas at the Art Gallery, then situated on Phillip's Square. I am afraid more attention was paid to the tea and gossip than to the works of art. One year there was a sketch of me in a large black velvet hat with black and white ostrich feathers, which roused my mother's wrath, as she did not approve of the artist!

Street hawkers wandered up and down the residential districts calling, "Any old clothes to sell" (and offering dusty plants in exchange), "Rags, bones, bottles for sale," "Tin ware to mend," "Scissors and knives to grind," and on hot summer days there was the boy who bawled "Strawberrees, strawberries . . . nice fresh strawberrees! 15¢ a box . . . two boxes for 25 cents."

Then there was the funny little old organ-grinder with his bushy beard and stocking cap (for all the world like one of Walt Disney's dwarfs), his ancient barrel organ slung across his chest with a broad leather strap and balanced on a wooden leg, wheezing out "The Last Rose of Summer" or "The Blue Bells of Scotland." He was followed later by the piano player murdering Traviata or "O Sole Mio." These paled into insignificance when the so-called German Band arrived and the children swarmed after it as though lured by the Pied Piper of Hamelin.

Street cars ran up Bleury street and along St. Catherine street to Guy street, and were drawn by two stocky horses, two more being hitched on going up hill. In winter there was a thick layer of straw on the floor and a little stove in the centre, and at intervals the conductor shook it and dust and ashes added to the discomfort of the passengers.

In summer there were open cars with 10 or 12 transverse seats and the conductor balanced himself on a narrow ledge and collected the fare as soon as the passenger was seated. Curtains of striped awning were pulled down when it rained but gave very little protection from the elements.

In summer a favorite pastime was to take a trip by boat to Laprairie, a delightful way to cool off, marred only by the myriads of shad flies that greeted us at the wharf. Another outing was to take the train to Lachine and "shoot the Rapids," a dangerous channel always piloted by an Indian from Caughnawaga.

In early days St. Lawrence Main street seemed to be the dividing line between the French and English, and Côte St. Antoine (or Westmount) was quite out in the country with only a few scattered houses and a "toll gate." Viewing Montreal today and particularly Sherbrooke street, it is hard to visualize its dignity and beauty 50 years ago. The fine stone houses set in large gardens with conservatories and stately trees made a wonderful setting for the winter Saturday afternoon meet of the Tandem Club.

Nowhere in the world could be seen more sumptuous turn-outs when they met at McGill Gates (not the handsome stone structure of today but simple wrought iron gates to that great university). The splendid high-stepping horses, the musk ox, buffalo or bear skin robes edged with scarlet or blue or green, the flashing harness and silver bells, some driving pairs, others tandem with an occasional "unicorn" dashing along the snowy packed road out to Peloquin's or Lumpkin's or across La Rivière des Pariries to La Maise . . .

The late-Victorian boyhood of W. G. Radford was the counterpart of Mrs. Ramsden's girlhood, and their two accounts share the same mood.

It was a period when boyhood seemed leisured, with time for walking about and looking at things. The street scene itself was like a theatre in its persons and props: the big jars of coloured fluids in the druggists' windows, the billboards, the grocer with his straw wristlets, the cobbler at his last, and the favourite cabman. As H. G. Wells wrote of this same period, it was possible to live "in the habitual enjoyment of such a widely diffused plenty and cheapness and freedom as no man living will ever see again."

W. G. Radford also pictures something now gone — the almost military preparation for Sunday, and the family moving like a battalion on a route march to and from church. He suggests that the combination of leisure and drill, of wandering and discipline may explain both the easy-going and the solid features of the late-Victorian's character.

These recollections are reproduced from the manuscript written by W. G. Radford after he had retired to Seattle, Washington. It was published in the column "All Our Yesterdays," in *The Gazette*, Montreal, July 24, July 31, and August 14, 1948.

This personal record is a story for Montrealers. Further, it is a story for Montrealers of a definite and ascertained vintage. It is for Montreal boys and girls who were born in the seventies and eighties, and, at the latest, the early nineties. . . .

Here, then, are the qualifications for initiation:

Can you actually remember the toll gate at the corner of Greene avenue and Sherbrooke street?

Did you ever hunt squirrels with a sling-shot on the Little Mountain?

Did you attend the High School (Big or Little) before the fire?

Do you remember when the horse-cars only ran to Greene avenue?

If you can answer these in the affirmative you are, at least, prepared to set out for a peep at the events that made the people of that period happy and feel again the atmosphere and environment that contributed thereto. . . .

The stores up and down St. Catherine street have shuffled down, and are only one or one-and-a-half story structures. The trolley wires, and most of the electric light and power poles, have disappeared. Slow-moving horse cars and horse-drawn traffic take the place of electric and motor vehicles. Pedestrians have all the rights and privileges, and seldom does any traffic move fast enough to interfere with a leisurely crossing of the street of anyone at any time in any place.

You look up Peel street and on your right stands the old High School — I mean the old old High School — and, if you approach closer, and look over the school yard fence, you will see the High School cadets on parade. It is a full-dress parade and the boys are in uniform — grey with black trimmings.

It happens to be the day of the O.C.'s inspection of the cadets and Major Macaulay and his officers are busily engaged. We might watch the inspection for some time were we not attracted by a slight commotion up the street in the neighborhood of Burnside, for the boys of the "Little High" are now being dismissed for the day. They noisily emerge from a small brick building in the rear of the "Big High." They are not old enough yet to join the cadets.

The destinies of the "Little High" are presided over by Mr. Sandy Shewan. The name "Sandy" must have had something to do with his complexion when he was a much younger man; for when we boys first met him, his hair and moustache were as white as snow. We certainly did not suspect it, and possibly Mr. Shewan himself did not, but there is no doubt about it that, even for those days, Mr. Shewan was one of the old school. He carried a strap in one pocket and candy in the other and dispensed each, either in accordance with his moods or the necessity of the occasion, and we were either wheedled or blitzed toward proper deportment.

In the "Little High" we had an absorbing and intriguing system of recording the progress of our studies. It was done by a system of "C" tickets and "R" tickets — the "C" denoting conduct and the "R" proficiency in recitation in our various subjects. You were given a set number of "C" tickets each morning and, in the event of misconduct during the day, you had to forfeit them. On the other hand, the "R" tickets were issued you during the day in each study, if your efforts and the results were considered satisfactory.

The game was to hold the "C" tickets intact and acquire as many "R" tickets as possible, either by fair or foul means. At the close of the day — in proper order from the head of the class to the foot thereof — you reported your spoils and dividends, which were duly recorded and you then surrendered all your tickets and made a fresh start the following morning. It afforded all the excitement of a progressive game and it, no doubt, encouraged acquisitiveness; but, when the "Little High" lost its identity, more improved systems of recording educational progress were adopted.

Boys walked to and from that school from as far away as Mount Royal Vale. One family of lads came all the way from Lower Lachine, driving a Shetland pony and dog cart. Well, here they all come tumbling out of the "Little High" and make their way down Peel street. They, too, watch the cadets on parade, for many of them have older brothers in the ranks.

We should keep our attention on two of these lads for a little while. They are brothers, and are probably satisfied with their "C" and "R" tickets for the day in question. Anyway school is over for the day and they hurry on to be engulfed in the great thoroughfare of St. Catherine.

But when they arrive at the corner they abruptly turn East to have a last long look in Miss Scott's confectionery window. The window is always well filled with shiny buns and colored cakes. You can obtain quite an assortment of Miss Scott's products for five cents and little short of a banquet for ten. The Misses Scott were kindly, pleasant, middle-aged ladies who wore long white aprons. Their hair was as smooth and shiny as their buns and they always exhibited the utmost of patience with their customers from the "Little High."

At school closing, after we had sung "Shoulder to Shoulder and Blade to Blade," our mothers would take us into Miss Scott's back store and we had ice cream, sitting at iron tables with marble tops. . . .

For a schoolboy in the year 1890 the area bounded by Sherbrooke, Dorchester, Peel and Greene embraced most of the then known world. . . .

So let us turn westward with the lads of the Little High School following the course of the sun, and see what may be in store for us. Our progress is slow, however, for immediately after crossing Peel street we have to stop at the window of Bryson's Drug Store and look into the large glass jars filled with colored fluids, in which you may see the reflection of the traffic in the street behind you — and upside down at that. . . .

There are very few stores on St. Catherine street west. What you pass on the way home is mostly rows of houses or vacant property. We shall have to stop for a few moments and look down into the bowels of the earth where men and machines are preparing for the foundation of Ogilvy's new department store. On and on we go. There across the street is Miss Murray's the florist, where we get a rosebud for our buttonhole for school closing exercises.

We have arrived pretty close to Mackay street by now and have taken a look at most of the things of interest on the homeward journey. St. Catherine street in those days was pretty well lined with bill-boards. In fact bill-boards seem to be one of the few institutions, that, in spite of their ugliness, have survived from those days.

In any event, the boys of the Little High found them as interesting as they were plentiful. From them we learned what was going on in the outside world — a world separate and apart from our own. We knew when Sarah Bernhardt, Lily Langtry, De Wolf Hopper, or the Great Hermann, were in town, or that "The Black Crook" was being played at the Theatre Royal and, young as we were, we realized that there was a similarity about the ladies that appeared at the Theatre Royal from week to week.

Well here we are at last at the corner of Guy and St. Catherine streets. We will have to stop and look around a little. Across the street is Mr. Jordan's grocery store, and beyond that a little is No. 10 fire and police station, and opposite that again is the cab stand. The corner opposite where we are standing, as you look south, is occupied by Mr. Turner's shoe repairing establishment, in the rear of which is the Count's livery stable, where you can hire out saddle or driving horses by the hour or the day.

It would be next to impossible to find anything today quite like Mr. Jordan's grocery store. Hams and bacon, sewed up in bright yellow cloth coverings, hung from the ceiling. Mr. Jordan himself wore an outing flannel waistcoat, long white apron from the thighs down, and straw or basket wristlets on the forearms of his shirt sleeves.

He did not devote all his time by any means to the grocery trade, for behind the store, running up Guy street, he had a yard and stables and was a breeder of fast horses and bull terriers. If you were lucky enough to be passing when the yard gate was open, you might see as many as a dozen to 15 bull terrier pups capering around the yard.

Turner's boot and shoe repairing establishment was a considerable social centre and rendezvous. Boys, and that type of men who did not seem to have any definite vocation, dropped into Mr. Turner's and watched him and his men at that most fascinating occupation of putting new soles and heels on old boots and shoes, while the news of the day and the gossip of the neighborhood were bandied to and fro. Mr. Turner himself is entitled to great credit for his interest in the community. He later became the sponsor of a boys' hockey team, "Turner's Tigers," to which he devoted considerable time and some financial support.

We have taken a look at the industries on two of the corners of Guy and St. Catherine street, those presided over by Mr. Jordan and Mr. Turner, and now we turn to the industry on the third corner, the cab stand. Before the days of the general use of the telephone, what music it was to our ears to be sent down "to the stand to get a cab." Of course, we had our favorite cabman: his name was "Barney."

There were certain ethics about the cab-stand profession that you were expected to observe: you really should take the first cab in the line and then the whole line of horses moved up automatically, and without orders from their drivers, and filled up the gap. But we used different tactics and spied out the situation from the other side of the street and we could spot his horse and cab from any other on the stand. We would cross the street, climb up on the box, capture, as it were, both Barney and his cab, and away we would go.

Barney had become endeared to us because he was an understanding and painstaking cabman. He welcomed both of us youngers on the box with him and he allowed us to drive the horse alternately. That box was pretty high up from the ground and to hold both of us on the box and generally supervise the undertaking was no easy job. However, it was good business on Barney's part for we always looked for him first and were quite disappointed if he were not on the stand and we had to make a second choice.

We first became familiar with Mount Royal from the box of Barney's cab. Parents, sisters, and babies inside the cab, with Barney, my brother and I taking general command on the box, we leisurely traversed the beautiful winding roads of the Mountain, past the reservoirs, up to the Lookout, for even children never tired of the enchanting view of the city, river and surrounding country.

Moreover, there was a treat in store for you at the Lookout Refreshment Room — if you had been good boys — and it was always the same treat, ham sandwiches and Gurd's ginger ale. Sometimes we took our tea to the pines overlooking the Mountain Ranger's gardens and sometimes we drove through the cemetery. We never lost interest in the firemen's plot, with its high column and a fireman in stone on the top.

On arriving back from one of these excursions, as he lifted me from the box to the ground, Barney presented me with a cabman's leather license. One of the metal numbers on it was missing but I treasured it for years, as both my brother and myself had decided that, when we grew up, we would be cab drivers.

What greater happiness could you have in life than sitting on the box of Barney's cab, driving Barney's horse along the roads of Mount Royal? . . .

Among the characters of this famous period was the "Tinware Man." He visited the neighborhood twice a week. He carried his entire plant with him — charcoal fire, box to sit on while doing his work, soldering iron, solder and resin. As soon as we heard him in the street crying "tinware to mend," we gathered around him and watched him by the hour, as the cooks and housemaids brought out various pans and utensils for him to repair.

As the autumn approached, the lamplighter, with his long torch to light the street gas jets, never failed to interest us. There was not much street illumination in those days, and when the Tuque Bleu Snowshoe Club was out on a tramp up the Mountain by way of the Gully, by what we would now consider as a feeble ray of a number of coal oil torches, we would be taken from our beds and wrapped in blankets so that we might see the winding streak of light on the mountainside, which was considered tremendously brilliant. . . .

The playground for the youth of the neighborhood was the "Haw Field" at the corner of Sherbrooke street and Côte des Neiges Hill. Right on the corner, outside the field, a couple of old ladies were established in business in the summertime, and here you could buy a ginger hand for one cent or a glass of spruce beer for one cent — reasonable prices when you bear in mind that it was on Sherbrooke street.

The entrance to the Haw Field was through a hole in the fence, made by removing one of the boards, and to this field the smaller boys of the neighborhood gravitated as soon as they could get away from parents, nurses or elder sisters. Some of the great footballers and hockey players of Montreal got their first introduction to sports in the Haw Field. It had its peculiar games; "tip and run" and "two in for bats" were favorites of our day. . . .

There was one day each week that St. Catherine street faded into insignificance and that was each and every Sunday. On that day Sherbrooke street and Dorchester street came into their own. That was natural, however, as St. Catherine street, with its street cars and occasional stores, was essentially a weekday street, and the Sunday crowds turned to other thoroughfares.

And in those days there certainly were Sunday crowds. Everybody seemed to go to church. Families seemed to swarm out of houses and Dorchester street was filled with people — aged, middle-aged, and youthful, making their way to church.

Considerable time on Saturday, and again on Sunday morning, was devoted to getting the whole family cleaned and shined up so as to present their best appearance on the Sabbath day. They walked in the street in pairs and the deportment was very correct. There was no loud talking or boisterousness. Almost on the same spot each Sunday morning you met other gloomy family platoons on the same errand bent. It was something like a battalion on a route march. There was a measure of discipline in the whole activity; there was no option as to attending, and you were "slicked and shined up" like a private in the ranks.

You walked a couple of miles; you listened quietly to long sermons and prayers that you did not understand; you reformed ranks and marched home again, observing the same decorum. After the Sunday dinner — when you were still on your best behavior — you paraded again to Sunday school, and to top the day off and give you an appetite for Sunday tea, you walked the length of Sherbrooke street.

It undoubtedly was a day of strict discipline administered by loving parents and I think it contributed to a bond of fellowship and satisfaction that discipline alone is capable of rendering. I have heard many men and some women complain that their outlook on life was warped by the fact that they were forced to attend church regularly in their youth in the Victorian days, and I have heard others advocating freedom of the choice of initiative of the youth of today.

But when I call to mind those Montreal Sundays, they do not seem to have spoilt the happiness of the times. In spite of their austerity and simplicity, they were part of a happy era and I believe, consciously or subconsciously, they contributed to whatever there might have been of character building in that generation.

Index

INDEX